What to Do
When Your Son or
Daughter Divorces

What to Do When Your Son or Daughter Divorces

DOROTHY WEISS GOTTLIEB
INEZ BELLOW GOTTLIEB
MARJORIE A. SLAVIN, M.S.W.

BANTAM BOOKS
TORONTO · NEW YORK · LONDON · SYDNEY · AUCKLAND

WHAT TO DO WHEN YOUR SON OR DAUGHTER DIVORCES
A Bantam Book / April 1988

LIBRARY OF CONGRESS
Library of Congress Cataloging-in-Publication

Gottlieb, Inez Bellow
    What to do when your son or daughter divorces / Dorothy
Weiss Gottlieb, Inez Bellow Gottlieb, Marjorie A. Slavin.
        p. cm.
    ISBN 0-553-34447-1
    ⌐1. Divorce—United States—Psychological aspects.
    2. Parents— United States—Psychology.   3. Adult
children—United States— Psychology.   I. Gottlieb,
Dorothy.   II. Slavin, Marjorie A.   III. Title.
HQ834.G67   1988   87-30827
306.8'9—dc19   CIP

Published simultaneously in the United States and Canada

Bantam Books are published by Bantam Books, a division
of Bantam Doubleday Dell Publishing Group, Inc. Its trade-
mark, consisting of the words "Bantam Books" and the
portrayal of a rooster, is Registered in U.S. Patent and
Trademark Office and in other countries. Marca Registrada.
Bantam Books, 666 Fifth Avenue, New York, New York 10103.

Our special thanks to:

Edith S. Engel, Co-leader of Group for Grandparents in Divided Families

Sally S. Green, M.S.

Geraldine Greene, M.S.W., Director of the Scarsdale Counseling Service

Willa F. Grunes, Ph.D.

Frieda S Herskovitz, Ed.D

Robert L. Sadoff, M.D.

Kevin Slavin, for his technical assistance

Contents

Introduction   1

1. We Were a Happy Family   5

2. Why Are We Taking It So Hard?   21

3. The Family Mobile   36

4. The First Months Are the Worst   47

5. Whose Side Are You On?   58

6. Do We Really Mean Come Home?   74

7. Money, Money, Money   90

8. There's No Such Thing As an
   Ex-Grandparent   114

9. Disturbing Disclosures   147

10. "Mom, Dad, I'd Like You
    to Meet . . ."   164

Introduction

What to Do When Your Son or Daughter Divorces is for the parents whose children produce more than two million divorces yearly in the United States. It is for you, who grew up expecting to face childbirth, marriage, and death, but never a divorce in your family.

This book is about your experiences as you contemplate the destruction of the much-repeated ending to the fairy tale: "and they lived happily ever after."

There is no "ever after" for the parents whose children decide to end a marriage. Though everything from too early toilet training to the women's movement is cited as the cause for the proliferation of divorce, no one simple answer suffices. Whatever the cause, parents are inevitably involved in the aftermath of the separation, and until recently no one seemed to be paying attention. TV, films, and books examined divorced men and women and their children, but their parents and their grandparents were not mentioned. There were volumes for divorcing couples and their children, but not a single one for the rest of the family. Nobody recognized that you might mourn the loss of your child's partner, might be confused about loyalty if you think your child is at fault, or even acknowledged that your child's divorce might touch you.

In *What to Do When Your Son or Daughter Divorces* we have pooled our personal stories and those we heard from parents, grandparents, divorcers, and children to provide routes of passage for the entire family. It is a handbook designed to move parents through the divorce process, with guidelines for the transition similar to those that help families with the passage from childhood to adolescence and to marriage. It is more *what to* and *when to* than *how to*.

We three collaborators have ourselves survived twelve divorces. Two of us have weathered six divorces among our collective five children, and one of us has seen two brothers each divorce twice and marry three times. One of us made her own divorce history.

From our vantage point as veterans of domestic battles, we feel we have the perspective that distance can bring. At least three years have elapsed since our respective breakups, and much of our family balance is restored.

In the first three chapters of *What to Do When Your Son or Daughter Divorces* we address the feelings you can expect to experience, beginning with shock and ending with acceptance or resignation. We analyze the grief period, why some parents get the blues and others say, "What's the problem?"

This book takes parents out of their sense of isolation and depression by showing how others who also mourned have responded. The shifts in family relationships that occur are also discussed, showing how the breakup of your child's marriage sets all the other family bonds astir, as on a mobile. We give options for some of the very practical questions that arise, such as money and loyalty. We bolster the instinctive responses that parents may suppress because they are unsure of the terrain of present-day divorce. We all know whose father pays for the wedding, but does that mean he should support his daughter when she walks out of her marriage?

So many things are suddenly different: the every-Sunday-morning phone call, family celebrations, and whether you are still "Mom" or "Dad" to your child's ex-spouse. Perhaps you are confused about how to deal with your ex-law and that whole ex-side of the family. Plenty of parents have a lot to say about that in our chapter on loyalty.

On a professional basis, one of us has worked with a unique group for grandparents in divided families at the Scarsdale Family Counselling Service. Through a newsletter and a telephone hotline at the agency, she has had contact with thousands of parents of divorced nationwide.

Even the parents who were glad the marriage was over, who never liked the in-law child, had concerns and questions. They wanted to know if their child's lawyer was representing him/her properly or whether to say hello to their ex-law's parents at a party.

Many, eager to tell their story, commented on the difficulties of sharing their now-quiet home with a divorcing, often disgruntled child. The divorcer often sees this resumption of an old living pattern as his or her prerogative, his right. Also, when it comes to money matters, there is real ambivalence among parents whether to give it, lend it, or withhold it. Their children frequently cannot understand why Mom and Dad worry about security or get upset over large, unpaid bills.

Those who are grandparents might have to serve as psychological caretakers of grandchildren during the grinding divorce period, their ballast in a treacherous sea. Grandparents get special mention because your child's divorce has much more at stake for you if there are grandchildren involved. You have to juggle between helping out and being used. Learn how other parents handled it when their grandchildren were instructed to ask them for day-to-day necessities that were their parents' responsibility. It could happen to you.

Being a grandparent usually brings continuing delights. However, when divorce occurs, grandparents are centered on the sadness of the grandchildren caught in the crossfire. While the parents focus on their own troubles, the child often has to face his tensions alone.

Recently we have noted a change regarding recognition of the parents of divorcers. There has been a good deal of news coverage about grandparents in divorced families who have sued for and won the right to see their grandchildren. Politicians have joined the bandwagon with the passage of a grandparents'-visitation resolution in Congress.

Some divorces we heard about had deep undercurrents of deviance, violence, or excesses of gambling and alcohol. Sometimes it was all a frightening surprise; sometimes families knew their child had a problem and hoped a good marriage would make it disappear. Chapter 9 gives specifics on how affected parents have confronted and handled these heavy-duty scenarios.

Like many who told us their stories, you and your child might confront hurdles to cross, disagreements to reconcile when it comes to his/her remarriage, differing on everything from stepchildren to multiple mate-changing. You might find yourself presented with a new mate before you have finished with the old one.

Although you have license to your own emotions, how you communicate them can make or break your relationship with your child. Many family ties strengthen as a result of riding these new waves together. This book helps point you and yours in that direction.

We talked to people all over the country from various ethnic and religious backgrounds, some with three BMWs and others who got around by bus. We found most respondents eager to tell their stories, different from 1980, when there seemed to be a conspiracy against talking openly about divorce. Names, places, occupations, and locations have been changed for the sake of confidentiality, but the stories remain intact.

Meanwhile, as you sort out the ex's and why's of your divorcer's shattered marriage, we will try to help you handle the challenge of change. The shape of your family will diminish for a while, but chances are it will expand again. Throughout each passage, your child will still be your son or your daughter; you will continue to be Mom and Dad. The family changes and the family remains the same.

1

We Were a Happy Family

The Bell Tolls

"Mom, is Dad home? Tell him to go to the other phone and you sit down."

Thus, your personal courier rings the alarm.

"Dad, take the phone. Bill has something to tell us."

All across the country, the bell is tolling. News of civil war in your home, in your family. You knew about divorce, read or heard about it in the media, but it was out there, somewhere else. Something inside you always intoned fervently, "Not me. Not mine."

The news of your child's divorce sets in motion an upheaval of feelings that will take months, sometimes years, to subside. The news is not just that there's a divorce but that you are shaken by it. "Why should I be upset? It's not my marriage," you argue. But you are deeply troubled. Divorce is one of life's most stressful events, and even though it is your child's divorce and not yours, you may be depressed, even tearful at times. Don't be surprised if you feel down and out. Many parents don't realize that the distress they experience at this time is actually grief and mourning, the same as you undergo when death hits your family.

Most parents in the past kept their feelings to themselves. They were unaware that the changes and losses occurring in the family were causing their depression. Mrs. Gardner, one of the persons we interviewed, age fifty-seven, went into therapy because she was sleeping too much and crying a lot. She wasn't doing her housework, she was barely getting to her secretarial job—which was only part-time—and she wasn't enjoying her food, let alone a night out with her husband. Mrs. Gardner thought she was going through a late midlife crisis or some sort of hormonal depression. Her feelings seemed to come from nowhere. She felt like a drag on her husband and a wet blanket with her friends. She did not realize how upset she was until she discussed her daughter's recent divorce with the therapist. Mrs. Gardner knew logically that the divorce was her daughter's decision, and she respected her daughter's feelings, yet she was out of touch with how it was affecting her.

Another parent, the father of three daughters, told us how much he enjoyed his first son-in-law. Here at last was the son he had dreamed of each time he paced the hospital floor. George was an ex-football player, a silent man like his father-in-law. They saw things in the same light, played golf on weekends, sat next to each other at the family table. The breakup of that marriage was a blow that sent the father reeling. He could not talk about his grief for a long time. It was not until he developed an ulcer and came to the attention of his doctor that disappointment came pouring out.

These examples are not farfetched. You can expect to feel depression and you don't need a doctor or a therapist to diagnose it. Divorce is the end of the couple, the end of the dream, the end of the myth that yours is a happy family. Even though the next chapter in your life and your child's may be better, you still have to write off this one, and you can't do that in one stroke. Not everyone experiences grief, but if you had an emotional investment in the marriage, you will be one of the many who do.

The parents we spoke with described three stages of their grief: the initial one, shock or denial; the reality phase, which included feelings of anger, guilt, failure, shame, and powerlessness; and, finally, acceptance. These phases are predictable and necessary for healing. They are part of the divorce process. You may experience some or all of the feelings in the reality phase, but not necessarily in any continuum of response. Grief is not an orderly process.

The Shock: It Can't Be!

Up to now you may have felt that your life has progressed through a somewhat regular sequence of family events. Your children were probably finished with school. That chapter was over. There were problems along the way, some of them frightening, but you and your children weathered them and moved on.

No doubt you felt, up to now, that everyone was relatively in place. Your kids were on their own, married or single. Your in-law child fit snugly into your family. You had reached a plateau. Maybe the married pair(s) made irritable remarks or shot warning glances back and forth, but when you all went out to dinner and everyone sat around the table laughing and talking, others looked admiringly at your happy family.

Even though you knew your children had areas of tension and insecurity, on the whole you felt satisfied that you had done a good job. Then you got the news! And no matter how you perceived your child's marriage up to now, the announcement of its death sends you into shock.

In the beginning, a numbness sets in. You say to yourself, "It can't be. Not to them! Not to us!" You weigh whether it could have been just a bad fight or whether they really mean it. You go back over the past, looking for signs you should have seen or did see, but still you don't accept the reality of the divorce. You try to pretend that nothing has changed, that they will patch it up. If you spoke to your daughter-in-law on the phone every week, you continue to talk to her. If you went out to lunch with your son-in-law regularly, you persist in the routine and discuss everything but the divorce. Nothing changes at first, because you don't believe it.

One couple recounted how their daughter and son-in-law came over, dropped the news on them, then the son-in-law went into the kitchen and helped his father-in-law fix the plumbing. Another couple described how their son and daughter-in-law called, insisted on meeting at a restaurant, told them the news between the soup and the broiled fish, and after dessert they all went out to see Woody Allen's *Love and Death*. These are some of the astonishing, but typical, examples of denial, on the children's part as well as the parents'.

Before long, however, something new happens. You invite them over for dinner and only one child shows up; or it is Father's Day and your son-in-law doesn't get on the phone; or your son shows you some mail from his wife's lawyer. Some symbol of reality hits you between the eyes and your adrenaline begins to flow. You thought it wasn't true? Now you know it *is*.

The Anger: It's Your Fault

The anger you feel may fall on any number of culprits. Throughout the coming months, you may blame your spouse, your in-law, your child, yourself, the other set of parents, any or all of the above. What you may be angry about is the dissolution of the family that was so important to you, and your powerlessness to put it back together. You look for a scapegoat, someone to blame.

Mrs. Maiman's recollection, though not typical, expressed her extreme anger and how she flailed about:

> I had a very bad time this week. My son's divorce is coming through and I think I let him have it. For a year I've been arguing with him but our relationship is very bad at this point. I told him I think he's a bad father to his children, and he's

selfish, and he doesn't think of anybody but himself. And at this point I need some help, maybe some counseling, because I feel this is going to put me down. I feel I just can't cope. By this time I should be *used* to it. My son's been separated for a year, but I'm always crying and my husband says if I don't do something I'll get a breakdown.

There will probably be many times during the postdivorce period when you'd like to speak your mind or let somebody have it. You struggle to suppress it, but there will be a new edge to your voice.

For a long period, possibly months, you will think almost constantly of the divorce. While you are driving alone in the car, you may fume about how easily the couple gave up. Why didn't they work out problems as they saw you do in your marriage? You went through tough times in your relationship but you kept your perspective and stayed together. They gave up without the effort you feel a marriage commitment deserves. You don't understand. Part of you disagrees vehemently. You stamp your foot on the accelerator and focus on your damaged hopes. Your daughter is thirty-five and may never present you with a grandchild. Your son's job may be jeopardized if he gets too upset over his marital problems.

Sometimes, during a wakeful night, you think about the coming change in your lives. Family habits such as visits and phone calls will be different, and so will family birthdays and holidays. Maybe you will waver about retirement or taking a vacation this year. Maybe you were just going to buy a car and suddenly feel you'd better wait and see. Who knows what checks you will have to write? You find it hard to make decisions. Will you have to take care of your grandchildren? Are you back to square one financially? Feelings swarm through you as you toss and turn, and you find yourself thinking, "How could they do this to me?"

It all depends who is telling the story, something like the six blind men describing an elephant in the Indian folktale. He's tall, he's short, he's lumpy, he's smooth; each one has his own version. The father of one male divorcer completely blamed his son. He said, "I know my son's temper and I'm sure he was hard to live with." (It's his fault.) The brother of this divorced man completely blamed the wife. "She was always a bitch on wheels. I never cared for her myself." (It's her fault.) The sister blamed the wife's parents. "They were always expecting her to have a bigger home, more luxuries. They were always pushing her to ask for more." (It's their fault.) And a friend of the family blamed the cousin. "When the wife saw her cousin get a much richer husband the second time around, she decided to end this marriage and seek her fortune with another man." Each critic ardently believed he was right. The funny thing is they probably all were correct, and the need to blame is human.

There may be some personal circumstances provoking your anger. One couple we interviewed was planning to retire. Mr. and Mrs. Matson had already applied to a retirement community in New Jersey and were planning to sell their house in New York, when their adopted daughter, Mary, came home with a baby. Mary had been on drugs during her teens and had never been very stable. She had barely finished high school, worked a little here and there, and ran off to California with Fred, who did odd-job carpentry work. Her parents were stunned when she appeared at the door with their only grandchild. They had such hopes when Mary married that her life had straightened out, but here she was, ready to move back into the house. The Matsons felt both responsible and angry, a combination many of you will recognize.

A common target of fury is the lawyers. They represent one side, one person, and their goal is to obtain what is best for an estranged wife or estranged husband. Courts of law set up sides and fuel the angers. Mediation is more conciliatory, but most divorcers make a beeline for the courts. Therefore, you too will probably join the ranks of those who complain: "The lawyers are making more problems." "They are charging too much." "Why is it taking so long?" Just as doctors are often blamed when there is a death, so lawyers are when there is an angry divorce.

Grandparents in divorced families who join support groups exclaim in anger and pain when an ex-law has custody of the grandchildren. Their chief complaint and cause for worry is that their grandchildren are not being raised properly. "Who is there when they come home from school? They're eating too many hot dogs, they're watching too much TV," were common laments. If their son had the grandchildren for weekend visits, they were distressed that he included his girlfriend in his activities or took them to an unsuitable movie. Some of their anxiety had a basis in fact, and the group supported these concerns. Nonetheless, they could laugh and agree that it was easier to figure out how their children could be better parents than how they could be good grandparents in these tangled divorced families.

We have been conditioned to suppress anger. It may be hard for you to admit it's there. You know intellectually that it is often irrational or unproductive to be angry at your child now. Still, if you aren't aware that it's part of the mourning process, you will be confused and feel you have lost control.

The Guilt: Mea Culpa Ad Nauseum

If you don't recognize your rage and allow yourself to express it, often it results in guilt. Unconsciously you say to yourself, "What right do I have to be exasperated with my needy child? It's not his/her fault. What kind of person am I, that I should be angry at a time like this?" This kind of guilt only cripples you and increases your resentment.

This is only one aspect of your feeling that you are to blame, that you are guilty. If your child is the one who decided to end the marriage, you may feel responsible for your rejected in-law, thinking, "We set an example for our son and expected he would love you forever." You were brought up to marry until "death do us part." You kissed and made up time after time for the sake of your vows and for the children, and you thought your children would follow your example.

If you find out that your child was sleeping in other beds, or drinking, or abusive, or acting out in any way by your standards, you are horrified and may be ashamed of her actions. If you could put into words the queasiness in your stomach, it might sound like, "What did I do wrong when she was young that she has turned out this way?"

Suppose instead you learn that your child is the one being abused. Suppose he has been putting up with an alcoholic, a drug abuser, or a gambler all these years and you never knew. Suppose, like a few people we interviewed, your child has been beaten, injured, almost killed. Then you will fault yourself for this too. "Was I so domineering a parent that my own child took such abuse and could not fight back?"

If several of your children are divorced or one child has confronted you with two or three divorces, then the weight on your shoulders is even heavier and you may try to place blame on your spouse: "Dad was away from the dinner table four nights a week, sometimes more." "Mother went back to work when the children were too young; they were left alone too much." These accusations are grist for the old-fashioned mom and pop fight that frequently occurs. Each one wants to save his own neck and be able to face the world with "It wasn't my fault!" Even if you are a single parent, you may point your finger at the "other" one's absence or the "other" one's genes.

Even if there are many separations or divorces among your family, your neighbors, and your children's friends, some sense of guilt may still surround you. You didn't want to join "that" crowd. Divorce might be the finís to marriages all around you, but your family is different. If you yourself were divorced, you hoped your child would not follow in your footsteps. You may feel that his divorce is a result of your past frailty.

When you were growing up, your parents probably would have reacted with more shame and less guilt. Divorce was traditionally considered disgraceful. If you had gotten divorced, they would have felt you were responsible for your own decision and your own life and would have expected you to survive on your own. Those of you who are part of the generation that raised children under the influence of Freud and Spock, however, believed that you had primary responsibility for your children's personalities. You lost sight of all the other influences on your child: his temperament, his talents and deficiencies, his siblings and other relatives, his special friends and teachers, the political climate of the time, the economy, and the attitudes, values, and power structure of the society in which he grew up. You weren't imbued with the current idea that personality and identity change occurs throughout the life cycle, but believed instead that your child's first five years in your safekeeping were crucial and immutable. Guilt goes deep in your generation and intensifies your response.

Whatever you did or did not do before the divorce, you can expect to doubt it now. If you stayed out of the couple's business, you will feel you should have been there more for them. You could have calmed your son down. You could have given your daughter advice. If you respected their independence, you will wonder now if you could have eased their marital stress. Should you have assisted them with the rent, volunteered to baby-sit more? Perhaps you did that and more; then what? You are now struck with a sense that you interfered: "Did we do too much? Should we have stayed out of it?" All those Sundays you had the children to dinner or all those evenings you baby-sat—perhaps your ex-law didn't like it or perhaps you made life too easy for the couple. Maybe if you had not tried so hard, they would have tried harder in their relationship. *Mea culpa ad nauseum.*

Since your parents and generations before them succeeded in keeping couples together, it's hard to believe there wasn't something you could have done differently. But remember, your parents lived at a time when family ties were more binding. Members were more dependent on one another financially and emotionally and generations lived in the same community, sometimes in the same house. Few families today have the controls of the neighborhood, religious institutions, or nearby relatives to bolster them and keep them together. Keep in mind, also, that in the past many marriages that were held together by nearby parents broke up after their deaths.

If your divorcing child has young children, it may make you wish you lived during an era when parents stayed together for the sake of the children. It is very hard to watch the struggle and sadness of your grandchildren as they try to cope with the divorce, and you will feel an overdose of guilt. You will wish there was something you could do to alleviate their anguish. There is, of course, a lot you can do to help your child and grandchildren—closeness, support, loving—but you will feel tempted to succumb to their more tangible requests, even when it's against your better judgment. You know that forty-dollar blue jeans will give only fleeting distraction, but you may buy them nonetheless. You hope that if you satisfy your grandchildren on that score, the separation won't bother them as much.

Your own prosperity is another thing over which you might reproach yourself. If your daughter is getting divorced and is adjusting to raising your grandchildren on a tremendously reduced income, then it's hard to enjoy your luxuries. How can you take pleasure in traveling or eating in expensive restaurants if your daughter and her children are scrimping to get by? These kinds of feelings may push you to help out financially.

Even though guilt has a bad reputation, it can help you to be altruistic, responsible, compassionate, and generally to rise to the occasion. On the other hand, if you wallow in it and don't recognize it as part of the mourning process, it can overwhelm you.

The Failure: "Divorce" Is Still a Dirty Word

No matter how your child protests, divorce represents failure to you. Even if divorce means your daughter is finally growing up and realizes her marriage is stunting her, it feels to you like she's shirking her responsibilities. Maybe it is a good thing that she is finally getting out of a bad situation or wants a happier union; still, you think she gave up. Whatever you know with your head, your heart tells you otherwise. Though she may call it growth or change, even she will agree, in a moment of confiding, that in some secret way she feels she has failed.

What frequently happens then is that unconsciously your child's failure becomes yours, and you set about to reform her. You do this not only because you care but because you would like to feel more successful as a parent. The reality is that your child wants to be treated with acceptance but does not want intrusion.

Frequently you lose confidence in her. After all, she made a mistake once, she could do it again. It is true that people learn from their mistakes, but then people often remarry only to find they create the same unhappy relationship again. If you have little tolerance for mistakes in yourself, you will have just as little patience with your child's blunder, assuming she has made one.

The Shame: Saving the Family Face

In 1980 there was a conference for grandparents in New York in which a woman stood up and said, "My son is getting a divorce and it's upsetting my marriage and I don't know who can help me." She was nervous and desperate, and it was obvious that it was easier for her to blurt this out to a room full of strangers than to confide in someone she knew. Several other participants owned up to having divorced children, while others spoke about grandchildren they've not seen since their child's divorce. At that time, parents of divorcing children were scarcely visible or accounted for, for they were too ashamed to talk about it. Because of their isolation they were unaware that what they were experiencing was common to others. They felt wrong, bad, and estranged.

Many parents still feel ashamed. We hear of those who cannot face family and friends after they learn of their child's divorce. A mother from the suburbs of Chicago no longer goes out in society because of her shame; an Italian-born couple, who care a great deal about appearances, has stopped attending family celebrations. We hope your experience will be more like that of the parent who confides her upset over the divorce to a friend, who answers, "Oh, no. You too?"

The Powerlessness: When You Can't Fight Them and You Can't Join Them

You have emotional power over your children, however grown up they are, and they influence you. You will always affect their feelings; they, yours. Whether your contacts are by telephone, when they visit, or at family gatherings, coming together always carries emotional history. You were once the voice of authority; they, your (more or less) obedient listeners. Think about your parents, if they are still alive. You are never so old that they can't push your buttons, make you respond if not automatically obey.

When it comes to your child's divorce, however, you are bound to feel powerless. You do affect the way your child feels about pleasing and displeasing you, but you can't alter what he or she does. This is because by the time they speak out, it is not to seek advice but to announce the news before too many others know it. They have made their decision and you have no chance to influence it. Pandora is out of the box and you really can't put her back.

You want to do something, not only because you understand, or because you feel like a failure, but because you are so helpless. This is one you can't "kiss and make better." You will probably ask questions, give opinions. That is a natural response. After a while you run out of homilies. You probably feel powerless in any of three ways: first, over the divorce; second, over what your child does next ("Help me, but don't tell me what to do!"); and third, over the pain of your grandchildren. They are so wounded and you would like to help them. You know your understanding and presence are consoling but insufficient against their overwhelming misery.

Acceptance: Stop Beating a Dead Relationship

Your grief may last from six months to two years, but sooner or later you will make your peace with your child's divorce. The shock will wear off, the family will restabilize, and you may find yourself admitting that something positive has come of it. A father talks about his son, divorced less than a year:

> When Jerry got divorced, Martha and I were beside ourselves. We were born in Austria and we just celebrated our forty-fifth anniversary. We don't believe in this kind of thing—divorce. But I have to admit, my son is looking better. He put on a little weight, a little meat on the bones, as they say. And he's going for his master's in business administration, which is a good thing. I always thought he should do that and I realize his wife held him back. She always wanted him to take her to swanky places, and at his age you can't be wining and dining and having a honeymoon forever, if you want to get an M.B.A.

Mrs. Dalton, a grandmother, also confessed to a change of heart. When her son got a divorce, at first she worried terribly about the grandchildren. Their mother was going to college, and the grandmother worried about who would take care of the children. She was a widow and would have offered to baby-sit, or to pay for a baby-sitter, but she was afraid her ex-daughter-in-law would see the offer as interference. A year later, she was visiting and had this to report:

My granddaughter is almost eleven now. She took me into the kitchen and showed me what she had made for dinner for Steffie and Mommy. She took me into her room and showed me the bed she had made. She was very proud of what she could do, and really very helpful to her mother. I had to admit I was proud, too. I realized then that there's more than one way to raise children. I think I was just mad and scared at first.

This is the kind of turnabout or balance we observed in parents of divorced children who had been healed by the mourning process.

We have found that other extended-family members experience grief, perhaps less intensely than parents, but grief nonetheless.

My sister made me very angry when she told me that she was getting a divorce. She went through every stage of her growing up in violent fashion. She smoked before anyone else her age and got in trouble at school, she stayed out so late that our parents were always scared that something had happened to her, and then they were furious when her key turned in the front door lock. I thought the separation and divorce were just a continuation of her acting out, but then I learned how miserably her husband had been treating her and what a stingy and insecure guy he was. Now she's settled with a man who is very nice and she is happier and it is easier for us to be friends.

It is quite possible that you and your family will see the day when you feel more detached from and impressed by the changes in your divorced child. Many parents reluctantly admit that their child looks better, acts more competently and maturely, and appears less nervous and more at peace. In addition, you, too, may ultimately benefit from the divorce. Many parents who pitch in as baby-sitters for the grandchildren or as fix-its in their child's house describe a rekindled sense of usefulness, closeness, and meaning in life.

Not everyone arrives at such a positive attitude. Some just get used to the divorce and learn to live with it. "I'd never tell Jim, but I think he made the biggest mistake of his life when he left Gwen. Their home was spotless, they had a warm group of friends, and their life was good," admitted one St. Louis father. After a while you will stop beating a dead relationship and get on with your life. Somewhere along the way, you will experience the inner quietude of acceptance or resignation.

True Divorce Goes On and On

One of the principal points in this chapter is to recognize that your reactions to your child's divorce are connected with grief. If you are mad or sad, blaming or ashamed, it is related to mourning. You will remain at the mercy of these emotions unless you understand this. You will react like the patient who went to the doctor with vague complaints of achiness. He didn't know if he was sick or tired. As soon as the doctor identified his symptoms as the flu, he felt less frightened and confused. Just knowing the source of your ache can make you feel more in control.

Knowing this should help you to understand our second point, which is not to fight against, avoid, or deny your feelings. Mourning is a necessary process for healing. By letting yourself feel and deal with the pain, it will ultimately come to rest.

Our third and final point is that divorce is not an event, it is a process. What you feel now will be old hat later on, a fact that was more obvious in our support groups than in our individual interviews. Members whose children had divorced one or two years earlier helped other, more agitated members whose children's divorces were more recent. The "older" members would say, "Oh, I used to feel that way, too, but I'm in a different place now."

Those who have gone before you suggest, however, that

there are certain milestones along the way that revive your grief, just when you think it is over. The separation is only the first milestone. After that you can expect the legal divorce to set you back. That is so much more final. Again, when your child moves out of the marital home and into the new house or apartment, there you go again. These developments, along with the fourth—the first holiday or family occasion—remind you that the shape of your family has changed. Divorce does not end with the tolling of the first bell, but goes on for a while.

Being aware of this should help you keep your perspective, even your sense of humor. As one parent said, showing us her album of family pictures, "My family is never boring. Every Thanksgiving I go through the most unbelievable suspense, wondering who's coming, who isn't. I take pictures partly just to keep track of who's together, who's not from year to year. Sometimes I'm disappointed, sometimes I'm pleasantly surprised."

2

Why Are We Taking It So Hard?

I don't know why my mother is taking it so hard. People get divorced every day. My mother and dad act like I had done something terrible, like it's a death in the family. Dad hardly talks to me. Susan and I just could not make it together. I am most unhappy not to live with my kids, but I'll see them as much as I can, and I'll support them, of course. What do my parents want me to do, stay in a marriage that doesn't mean anything to me anymore? Why don't they come into the twentieth century?

—Don

What can we do, Julie, we've never had a divorce in our family. My father must be turning over in his grave. I never expected Don and Susan would come to this. Did you even suspect it? I thought our kids would stay happily married like we did. Didn't you? What went wrong? And those little ones, what now? We were good parents and we had good kids. Why should we be in this trouble?

—Dad

You're Not Okay, I'm Not Okay

Some parents sail through the divorce(s) of their child seemingly unscathed. This is usually the case if both of the divorcers are already involved in new relationships, or if the parents disliked their in-law child, or if they felt the marriage was not a good one. Such parents may come from a tradition of divorce, so for them it is quite commonplace. The affluent, the "beautiful people," seem more accustomed to and sanguine about the changing of partners. Perhaps this is because, in many cases, the wives have incomes of their own and their life-styles are not jeopardized because of the separation. They discuss divorce like this: "You remember Bertie, he was Ellie's second husband. I liked him, but then I liked Alan, too."

Parents who take divorce easily have experience and precedent to follow, and in many ways that makes it easier. They know, because they have lived through it before, that there will be other marriages, other divorces. They have guidelines to steer by.

Then there are parents who experience their child's divorce as though it were happening to them. Psychologists call them "fused" with their child. When they feel cold, they think their child feels cold; when they are hungry, they think their child is hungry. They have the "you're not okay, I'm not okay" syndrome. These parents do things for their child instead of for themselves, just as George did, who had spent his life making sacrifices for his daughter. When she was going through her divorce her pain was his pain, and her heartbreak became his heart attack. He almost died because he could not separate his life from hers.

Gertrude's mother lived through her daughter and organized her life around Gertrude. "After she got married I called my daughter every morning. We talked over our problems, mostly hers. We were close when she got married and left home. We would lunch together at least three times a week at her house or mine. Sometimes we went to a restaurant. I sewed clothes for her kids and told her how to cook certain foods." When Gertrude divorced her husband, it was the first time she did what she wanted instead of what her mother wanted. "How can you do this to me?" her mother wailed. And, "She never told me she was that unhappy with Leroy."

There are many parents who lead their own lives, involved in their work or their interests. They are on the go a great deal. These parents feel fulfilled in their later years and see their children's existence as very separate from theirs. As grandparents they hug and kiss, but they do not baby-sit or take vacations with all the kids. If you feel that way, you probably take your children's divorces with less agony, even with equanimity. "I don't see why all this fuss about parents. My son is divorcing and my daughter-in-law and I are still on speaking terms." That mother never pretended, or wanted, to have more than an in-law relationship with her son's wife.

Your response will settle somewhere between comfortable and upset-and-can't-fathom-why. There are reasons why some parents take it hard and some take it in stride. In the first chapter we talked about the things you have in common with other parents of divorcers, reassured you that what you feel is to be expected during this crazy time. Now we will explore how and why some of your responses differ from those of other parents.

We Don't Believe in Divorce

If you come from a deeply religious background where divorce is deemed sinful, you may indeed go into a kind of bereavement when it happens in your family. You don't want to go to church or synagogue and face what you perceive as censorial or pitying looks. A sense of shame invades your life, as though it is you who have "sinned." You find it hard to talk to relatives on the phone or to attend family functions. You want to hide from it all. Jews, Protestants, Catholics, Quakers—some of each among those we talked to—felt real pain. If the above description fits you, you believe your children's marriage vows, like yours, are holy, taken under God. To break them is sinful. "I could not bring myself to tell anybody the news of the separation for a long time. We are religious people. Divorce is condemned like birth control and abortion. We take one partner for life, for better or for worse," said one parent with whom we spoke.

Mrs. Moynahan, the mother of a divorcer, tells of the consuming shame a religious parent feels: "We sent Reggie back to his wife, where he belongs, but he did not stay. I told my cousin, who is close. I hoped she would break the news to the rest of the family. I just couldn't touch it. She must have told everybody. Some called to say they were sorry. Some said Joe and I should make him go back to stay. Some did not call at all, and that was the hardest. I'm not sure I can face the family Christmas party this year."

In many strongly ethnic or religious groups, the survival and continuance of the family are not just a priority but an absolute. If you are part of such a group, divorce is anathema to you, to your family, and to many of your friends.

Steve Leone was a compulsive gambler. He followed the horses avidly, and even at home he kept the radio tuned to the race results. No money was sacred—the food, the mortgage—and collectors were always calling. His wife Lil was embarrassed and frightened. Every morning when he left the house she assumed he was going to his business, and it was only when the business went bankrupt that she realized the extent to which he had been gambling and diverting the company money to the racetrack.

Lil was so devastated that she contemplated suicide. She went to her mother and said she was getting a divorce. Her mother reminded her that it was a wife's duty to stay with her husband no matter what. Lil was distraught and went to a marriage counselor. She took Steve with her for the session. He confessed that he had not only gambled but taken drugs and had extramarital affairs. Yet, Steve wanted the marriage very much, and he swore that he had finished with all that. He agreed to go to Gamblers' Anonymous, counseling, and whatever else his wife wanted him to do. Lil still really wanted a divorce, but she had no income to fall back on, and tradition dictated that she stay put.

Her family organized to oppose her divorce. Lil's mother sent her brother Mark to talk to her. He spent an entire exhausting day persuading Lil not to kick Steve out. Lil had already packed his bags and taken her husband's house key from him. After ten hours of Mark's harangue, she agreed to try the marriage one more time. When Steve resumed his former ways, Lil got out before her family could send another mediator to persuade her to stay.

Her family had mobilized to oppose the divorce, but when they realized Lil's justified determination to go through with it, they supported her decision. The family was there to supply living quarters, food, and enough spending money to keep her off welfare. Lil survived, started a catering business, and eventually made a happier second marriage.

We don't mean to imply that only deeply religious people or those from strong ethnic backgrounds take divorce hard or put a high value on the family. Among the many people we interviewed, WASPs reflected as much sorrow as any other group, but their "stiff upper lip" tradition makes it less visible to the naked eye.

What'll I Do When You Are Far Away?

What'll you do? You won't be quite so distressed. When your married children live many miles away, your intimate involvement with them is diluted by the distance between you. There is the telephone, but, though you may get hints of how their lives are from the frequency of calls, there is much that inevitably eludes you. Your perceptions depend on where things are at the moment they pick up the phone. Long distance may have shielded you from their problems. They hoped the distress would disappear before you visited, or assumed that what you didn't know wouldn't hurt you. That is not to say that your parent ears are not attuned to sounds of strain in your child's voice. You can sense a lot from voices, but the combination of voices, facial and body expression, and the frequency of seeing each other in the flesh communicates more.

Besides, being far from family, your children have built up some independence out of necessity, since they can't run to you when things get rough. Most out-of-towners have a network of sympathetic neighbors who become like family in many situations. Whether they need support for emergencies or familiar faces at holiday tables, they rely on their network of friends. These children cannot share as much of their lives with you as they might if they lived down the street.

You just are not as involved with the children who live far away as you might be if they lived nearby. Surely, there are long visits, but the attempt to cram so much love into a concentrated period of time sets up its own tensions. Phone conversations with your grandchildren range from a weak "Hi," the most intelligible comment from a two-year-old, to a long chat about teachers, friends, and the pressing need for a certain T-shirt from a ten-year-old. Whatever the texture and frequency of the phone calls or the visits, your life has less of that family feeling than it would if they lived near you. You do feel a sense of loss at not seeing and sharing many stages of their growth, but the detachment can help you through tough times.

Conversely, when the divorcers are part of the warp and woof of your day-to-day life, divorce hurts more. You have sensed the early signs of malaise in Mom, Dad, and the kids. You may have already worried through several episodes that hinted at the shakiness of their family, as this couple did:

We kind of knew it was coming, but didn't want to believe it. Sometimes when they came for Sunday dinner Mims and Eric were at each other, and the kids seemed tense and Eric yelled at them a lot. We know Mims hated us to see this. She doesn't believe in airing dirty linen, especially in front of us. We hadn't been sure Eric was the one for her when she was dating him and said so. She wanted to prove to us that she had been right about marrying him. We would not let ourselves think about separation and divorce, but it happened right under our noses. It's hard to watch the disintegration of your child's life. You feel partly responsible somehow, and that you must help, being right there.

Being "right there" on a regular basis and seeing the little erosions in the relationship (and the big ones) keeps you continually nervous and on edge. You are worn thin, and the shock of the reality is both confirmation of what you feared and a hit on the head!

The Bigger Ones Can Call You Themselves, the Little Ones Can't

Among the matters that perturbed Mims's parents, as well as many others we talked to, was what would happen to their grandchildren. They kept a watchful eye many days and discussed their concerns many nights, but since Mims had custody, they were not worried about when and how they would see their grandchildren.

> We were sure that Mims would have custody of the children so we would not lose contact. That was the one bright thing in the whole picture, or at least that is how we felt in the beginning. Now we see that the three of them, our daughter and her kids, are getting along okay. She makes pretty good money, and with our help and Eric's child support (when it comes), they are not in financial trouble.

If you are on the noncustodial side of the divorce decree, you stand to lose more, hurt more, and take it harder. You are in the most powerless position. The divorce of a nearby child who has small children, when you are on the wrong side of custody, produces the greatest trauma for parents. These three factors—distance, young grandchildren, and having your child only a sometime-parent—account for the largest percentage of grandparents who seek support groups to help them through. If you fit into all three categories, don't despair. Your family can rebalance in spite of it, but you have more at risk—hence, you take it harder—than other parents of divorcers.

> We went through a bitter divorce with our eldest son three years ago. Of course, we sided with him all the way, and the custody fight was such a nightmare. He gave up fighting completely and started a new life in California. Now our ex-daughter-in-law is making us pay the price for our loyalty to our son. We are forbidden to visit or even see our grandchildren, now eight and five and a half years old. We drove out to their school one day, desperate for a glimpse of the boys. We telephoned to ask if we could come to the house. She said, "No, no way!" We left the Christmas presents at the door; they were returned unopened, just as were the birthday presents we sent. We are distraught.

This desperate grandfather, a banking executive, typifies the most aggrieved parents of divorcers. He tried every avenue to see his grandchildren. He called the other set of grandparents and asked them to intervene. He consulted his priest. He and his wife went to a family counselor, but for a long time he felt, in more ways than one, at a dead end. Well-meaning friends told him, "Don't give up. One day, when your grandchildren are big enough, they will get curious and seek you out on their own." He said, "Who can wait? My wife has a heart condition and I have high blood pressure. We're not so young, you know."

It is one year since that grandfather and his wife went to court to obtain visitation rights, and once every two months they are allowed to talk on the phone with their grandchildren and to send them birthday and Christmas presents. In time, their ex-law's vindictiveness might abate, and she might send the children to visit them.

If your grandchildren are old enough to call you or write to you, they may do that, or they may be too "brainwashed" about your "wickedness" to do either. With younger ones there is only a vacuum if you can't see them or even talk to them on the phone. You are caught in the agony of the realization that you may never get to know them, nor will they know you.

There is something unnatural about grandparents in divorced families having to prove the right to see their grandchildren. You would think that, unless they were violent or alcoholic, they could take for granted their connections by birth. A grandchild who felt he should be able to take for granted the bond with his grandparents recently wrote, "Some grandparents push food in you. No matter how big you are, they'll say you are too thin. Grandparents try to make you happy. They believe you. They rub your back. Maybe you just go out to arcades and sleep over and talk and be close. . . . A kid should not be kept from his grandparents just because his parents don't get along. But sometimes that happens." (From *The Leader*, Corning, NY, 12/24/83.)

You Gave Him Your Love and Now You Can't

Second to feeling alienated from your grandchildren is the loss of a loved ex-law. If your in-law was as close to you as your own child, you will suffer from the divorce. If you loved your in-law child because he was "the dream guy" in your daughter's life, or was the mate you felt was right for her, or was the son you never had, it is harder for you to feel neutral about him or to actively dislike him. You feel more deeply the loss, the empty spot in your family. It would be great if those who loved one another could keep their deep attachment after the divorce, but usually that doesn't work. You can still be good friends, if your child is willing, but the breakup sits between you in spite of yourselves.

She's Getting Married in the Morning

You may be glad when your ex-law decides to marry again. It takes a burden from your son, emotional and financial. If you and she have a good rapport and she seems happy at the prospect of her new commitment, you will feel good about it, too.

If you were deeply involved with your grandchildren now in her care, there could be jolts ahead. You baby-sat, provided swimming lessons, took them on vacations, and came home exhausted. You were glad to pitch in and glad to pitch out. When your ex-law remarries, her new husband may feel uncomfortable with you, see your ministrations as meddling, and not want you "hanging around." A Baltimore grandfather tells this story:

> I live alone. I enjoy my grandchildren very much. It goes without saying that I love them and they love me. When my son and his wife divorced, she got the kids. I figured I'd keep communications with her open, so I'd take the kids to the park on the Sundays my son didn't have them. I would also help around the house, put washers in the sinks, fix broken toys, things like that, whatever I could do to help. I'm a doctor and they turn to me when they fall off their bikes or something hurts. My ex-daughter-in-law and I got along fine. I stayed with the children evenings when she went out. My grandchildren liked my bedtime stories about "the olden days." Now she is getting married. Her boyfriend doesn't seem to want me around, and she goes along with him. I'm afraid I am going to lose contact with those kids.

Even though you are on good terms with your ex-law now, the terms can shift with her remarriage. They can shift when your son remarries as well, but in a different way. This time your ex-law may be jealous and take it out on you. The courts are full of grandparents who helped rear their grandchildren, only to be turned out following a remarriage.

There are possible ways out of this bind, if it is your ex-daughter-in-law who is wedding. If you can come to an understanding about what is best for her children—your grandchildren—you have a fighting chance. New partners bring new challenges. The children might need your attention even more, or less, but this is the time for you to be creative and flexible.

Picking up the Pieces

If you perceive your child as weak, hurting, or needy, you will suffer from the breakup of his or her marriage more than if you think of him or her as strong. There is an old saw that a mother carries the weakest child closest to her heart. It seems logical that parents worry more about a dependent child than an independent one. You feel for her, with her. Her hurt and confusion are so visible and palpable you can't ignore them. You tend to do more for her than you might for a stronger child in the same boat. Be careful: don't push her back into the dependency of a little child. She has already shown that she can function well enough as an adult to take on the responsibility of marriage. She can handle the divorce shock too, with a small assist from you.

Joe Gordon describes his son:

> Sam was the one we were always concerned about. He didn't do too well in school and didn't get into the college of his choice. He wet the bed until he was six. We thought it was because he was a middle child squeezed between a very bright brother and an appealing little sister. When he married Joan we were thrilled. We thought they were great together, and he seemed to grow into a stronger person with her. We tried not to interfere in their lives too much, not to encourage him to complain to us as he had done in childhood. Then, boom, Joan left him, and we seemed to have our "little boy" back. All his maturity seemed to fall away. It's doubly hard to take because we thought he had really grown up. He seems to need us so much now!

Remember, he is not a "little boy" anymore. He may regress for a while. Be assured he will put himself back together again, as this girl did:

> We were so impressed with our daughter Jill. After they married, she worked in an office to help send Chris to medical school. She put off having children. We helped too and were all so proud to call Chris "Doc." Of course he wasn't home a lot during that time. When he was home, he was "hitting the books." We thought he'd be so grateful and loving to Jill for her financial and emotional support. The first years of internship were hard on her. She was home alone a lot. At last he got a good position in a hospital and we thought they would do great. After a year, he left home. It was as though he didn't need her anymore—or us. We are devastated.

This is an example of a mother feeling that her child was treated shamefully after she had worked to give her husband his heart's desire. That kind of divorce can be particularly devastating to parents. However, there is a happy ending to this story: Jill remarried happily and has children now.

You may be the kind of parents who are more troubled by a daughter's divorce than by a son's. You feel she has fewer options. Despite the women's movement, it is still men who are expected to take the initiative for dating. If your daughter is basically reticent, that leaves her home many nights, and often sets you to looking for eligible men for her. As you look around and survey "the scene," you see men with women much younger than they are, and your daughter suddenly seems "too old." You think she may never marry again. Give her time. She will meet a new mate on a plane, at work, or in her next apartment. Don't get frantic and push her too hard. She may not feel ready for a new relationship yet, like this young divorcee:

> My parents are taking my divorce so to heart. They worry when I'm home after work, they fret when I am not. You'd think I was

twelve instead of twenty-six. I often feel lonely, but my friends (lots of them divorced) and I go out for dinner and concerts when our schedules coincide. I am not anxious to date just yet. I want to go slow. I wish Mom and Dad wouldn't look as though the sky has fallen. I am going to be okay.

Sons can hurt as much as daughters, and may be as weak, miserable, and needy as their sisters. This mother seems to handle her anxiety well:

Bob is so despondent. Judy meant so much to him. Now he is lost without her. She was his "golden girl," pinned in high school. We don't even know why the marriage failed. He asks very little of us except to be left alone. We ache for him and with him. We are just standing by, ready to help.

Bob's mother is wise to stand by rather than scurry to fill the void for her son. He needs time to go slowly.

Your Child's Attitude Makes a Difference

While you are observing, judging, and trying to be supportive of your divorcer, he has at least one eye on you. If he thinks it's fine for you to see his ex-wife and you and she would like it that way, then the divorce will be easier to handle. If his desire for loyalty demands that you have nothing to do with her, and you want to keep in touch with her, you will probably take it harder.

This sixty-seven-year-old widow from New Jersey was distraught due to her son's attitude:

Kate, my ex-daughter-in-law, called and invited me to dinner. I love her and she loves me, and it's my son John who ended the marriage. He thinks I'm plotting with Kate against him. He said, "When are you going to realize I just don't love her anymore?"

He doesn't understand. Kate's lonely and I'm lonely, too. I don't see why he should get upset if we have dinner together now and then.

Parents whose children are less angry or threatened are more fortunate than this ex-mother-in-law. They are freer to follow their own inclinations about their ex-laws. Your child's attitude certainly makes a difference in how you look at the divorce.

Who You Are Affects How You Are

You and your family take your cues from your child in the way the separation and divorce are affecting him or her. But who you are and who is or is not beside you are strong elements in your immediate response.

Those of you who are married have someone with whom to share the experience. It is always helpful to go through a shocking experience with someone else, but it can also have its disadvantages. You may worry about how to inform your spouse if he has a history of heart trouble. You may find ancient differences between you awakened by your child's divorce. You may be frustrated because you want to get away and your wife wants to stick around to help. Being married is no guarantee that your child's divorce will be easy, but usually it is one more event you and your spouse go through together that strengthens the bond between you.

The relative ease with which divorced parents accept their child's divorce is well illustrated by this divorcer, Alice Thompson, a forty-five-year-old-woman whose youngest child just entered college. When she and her husband Raymond decided to separate, Alice said, "I had no difficulty telling my mother. She and my father were divorced, so she understood. Even though she liked my husband, she said, 'Do what you have to do, Alice.' And we've never even had to discuss it further."

Alice's husband had a much tougher time of it, however.

Raymond's mother was a widow, and for several months he and Alice kept up the charade of marriage in her presence. For quite a while they continued to go to her house on Sundays, as had been their routine, although they were living in separate apartments.

Not every couple elects to protect a widowed parent from the shock of their divorce, but our interviews suggest that widows have the hardest time dealing with the news. They feel alone with their grief and confused about what to do. As Raymond reported, after revealing his separation to his mother, "Even though she's glad my father was spared having to face this, I can see she is upset. If he were alive, she could ask him whether to call Alice, whether to do my laundry, things like that. This way she's so upset she doesn't talk to anyone."

Most of the people we talked with were disturbed and confused over their child's divorce. A few were accepting. Married or divorced, your children present ups and downs, and married, divorced, or widowed, you must face it.

3

The Family Mobile

Who Can Define Family?

Family means the people you can count on, no matter what, the comforting thought that you always have your place at the table, even if you are not there to claim it. Family means the people who share tons of stories—fussy, ugly, warming, sad—but all with very familiar people as central characters. Family means knowing you will be invited to weddings and are expected at funerals; that you'll show up when a member is in the hospital or needs some kind of support. It means people glad to greet each baby, whose birth makes them feel secure about the future of the tribe and gives them the chance to play "Whom Does He Look Like?". It means joyful meetings with and painful partings from relatives at buses, planes, and trains; it is holidays, parties, meals together, hugs, tears, fights, jealousies, and comfort.

Family is a powerful icon for those who lack such a network as well as those who have it. We all would like it to be there for us always, even as we acknowledge that close living and sharing can produce anger, jealousy, fierce competition for attention, and the recognition of shared traits that we hate in ourselves and our relatives.

Family is an invisible system of who does what to whom and who has power over whom. As your children grew up, you negotiated many matters: when baths were taken, TVs shut off, and how long the bedtime story lasted. Later, larger matters were put on the table: college selection and the sex of the roommate your child brought home. With all the intimacy and caring, there was inevitable conflict between you and your children. Growing up, each of them struggled not to depend on you or your values too much. They opposed one another, too. Through each battle, yours and theirs, you all tried to hold on to the imaginary string that kept you joined together.

Just as when your children married you could feel that imaginary string stretch, so when they divorce you can feel it shrivel. The family expands and contracts with every addition or subtraction of a member. When divorce strikes your family, through your child, the alliances and divisions throughout the entire extended family shift, even break.

When divorce occurs and you experience so many pushes and pulls on near and dear relationships, it is useful to think of your family as a mobile. If you cut the string between any two parts, it unbalances the whole structure, until it is repaired. Your whole family reverberates when your child divorces and the mobile goes on tilt.

In our interviews we found that divorce affects the closeness between you and your spouse, you and your child, you and your in-laws, and you and the other set of parents. It also affects the relationships between you and your other children, and you and your grandchildren; just about every relationship on the family mobile is touched by the disruption.

You and Your Spouse

This is a story of the Cranes, a couple in their late forties:

> Joe and I had a pretty good marriage. We did most things as a pair and laughed a lot. (Cried, too.) Sure we argued. I would call him on some point, he would get angry, and I would back down. I love him and figured it wasn't worth a big row. I mostly just get

quiet rather than face an issue. Usually we differed on how to spend money and how to raise the kids. He wasn't too tolerant when they disobeyed, but if they needed anything material he always came through. He was always a good provider, and still is.

When our middle daughter married, we gave them a nice, but not lavish, wedding. They seemed fine for a while, then the marriage went sour. We never knew just why. I thought we should stay out of it but Joe was of a different mind. It was important to him when B.J. married that she had never slept with anyone else. He still believes that her husband should be the only man she ever sleeps with.

He tried to get them to go to a marriage counselor, even offered to pay for it. He would tell me I was a neglectful mother and that's why our daughter B.J. was having trouble. I accused him of meddling and making things worse. Sometimes I'd say, "You aren't such a great father either!" and then go into my silent routine. When the kids separated, Joe kept in touch with Dan, our son-in-law, offered to help him in any way he could. He tried hard to keep the marriage together. He thought divorce was a disgrace and that B.J. couldn't do better than Dan.

Well, the kids got divorced anyway, but the strain of that year and a half put a crimp in our marriage that doesn't seem to iron out. We don't laugh as much, go out the way we did.

Divorce raises differences that go deep into the family core. The strain the Cranes experienced over their daughter's divorce brought out their characteristic ways of handling disagreements and antagonized their relationship. After two years of upset, they settled back into their comfortable pattern and weathered the stress.

Their story may have some elements similar to yours and many that are different, but it illustrates the kind of disruption your child's divorce can cause between you and your spouse. Often both parents feel the same pain but handle it differently. One would like to keep in touch with the ex-law "for the grandchildren's sake"; the other never wants to see "that idiot" again. One is willing to meet his son's new girlfriend; the other insists, "If that slut sets foot in this house, I'm leaving!" You both know it's a distressing situation but can't agree on how to handle it. You would like to support each other but can't always do so. In spite of your arguments, chances are you'll get through this and dance together at the next wedding.

When parents don't reconcile their differences over their child's divorce, their angers and frustrations can crack open their own marriage. They, too, may split apart, throwing the family mobile into greater imbalance. Untangling those invisible strings after two divorces and getting the mobile stable again makes the rebalancing act harder on everyone in the family. The wear and tear may be severe, and it may take years to repair, but it can be done.

You and Your Child

This is the story of the Lances, a couple in their middle fifties:

> Since our son and his wife, Sandy, split their household, we see a lot more of Josh. He calls us more, ostensibly to see how we are and then to tell us how he is. He stops in at the end of one of his hardworking days and often stays for dinner. That pleases my wife. We do worry about him more than we did when he was married. We're not sure he is eating properly or sleeping well these days. I think he's lonely. Sandy has the children except for weekends.
>
> Josh and I often discuss his legal and financial situation, two lawyers talking. That gets us into areas of his life I never knew about. I am very angry with Sandy. She was impossible during the divorce process and used the kids, my grandchildren, as a weapon, a bargaining chip. She still does, every chance she can get. I don't see any point criticizing her to my son, but if he starts it, I chime in. I can't help it.

We've started to play squash together. I look forward to those hard-fought games. Maybe my wife is a little jealous of my new closeness to my son. She feels left out, but I think she understands and rejoices, too.

The tilt in the Lances' family mobile is probably temporary. The chances are that for a year or so Josh will feel more need to be close to his parents. They represent a refuge during the first months after divorce. However, before long he will start spending more time with friends, seeking companionship, a new mate. Mom and Dad may feel rejected as he moves on. If their lives are full and they keep their perspective, they'll know that this is the right way for Josh.

The Lances' story is a positive one in many ways, but it can all go in another direction. You may feel angry at your child for the shame, embarrassment, and disappointment you experience. You may feel your child could have lived in the style you had hoped for her, but now she has given it up. You may think she should have stuck it out. You can't support her in the style to which she has become accustomed, nor do you think she can earn enough to pay the kinds of bills she likes to accumulate.

You probably don't want to distance yourself from your child, and likely you intended to hide your hostile feelings. If you find yourself giving unwanted advice, that could be your anger coming out indirectly. In response, your child may either attack or withdraw from you. What you are saying is that he doesn't know how to handle his life, and that you know better. You are seizing a second chance to remake your child. You can't, and this is certainly not the time to try.

Before, during, or after divorce, some parents get blamed. If your daughter married right out of the fold, this divorcing period is the first time she has examined her own separate values, not yours, not her husband's. If your son married someone a lot like you, his divorce from her may mean he can't face you because you remind him of her. This can be painful, puzzling, especially since this backing off happens most often in children who have been extremely close to a parent. In such cases, Mom or Dad brings back memories of the missing mate. If your child begins therapy during this period, you may be targeted as vipers temporarily while she works through her problems. This may mean greater distance or negativity between you for a while, but when your relationship rebalances it will have a truer basis.

You and Your In-Law/Ex-Law

Your ex-law's exit from the family leaves an empty spot. You may be more reluctant than your child to give up the relationship. When your child married, many of you embraced the in-law child as your own. Now you are expected to give him up without a whimper, ignore the imbalance of the mobile. If your child does not object, you could continue to be friends, but sooner or later the relationship usually ebbs.

A divorced daughter whose father died a year after her breakup said, "I feel partly responsible. I really feel Dad died of a broken heart. He could not handle the divorce. My father loved Bill from the moment I brought him home for approval. I couldn't get Dad to talk about his loss. He kept it bottled up inside. His reaction was extreme and fatal!" Some parents have called the divorce an amputation. Others were forced to stop loving their ex-law: their child insisted on it. There were some parents who withdrew because the ex-law seemed so changed. "I can't understand my ex-daughter-in-law. She used to be full of laughter and now she is icy and indifferent. It's as though she is two different Helens," said one mother. A father-in-law lamented, "We always hoped that he loved us, not because he had to, but because he wanted to." If you are taking the loss to heart, it is very likely that your pain will ease in time.

The separation process is less hurtful for those whose ex-laws keep in fairly close touch with them. These parents usually remain involved as long as their own child remains single.

When that child remarries, which often happens within three years, the parents lose interest in the ex-law. It is as though there isn't room on the mobile for both wife and ex-wife or husband and ex-husband.

One anguished mother told us, "After the divorce Hedy used to come to see me with my granddaughter. I loved those visits. My ex-daughter-in-law is a liberated woman and I always enjoyed talking to her. I learned a lot about all the options open to women now, that I never dreamed existed. Since I only had three sons, she was my first sense of what having a daughter was like. I loved it. When Carl remarried I felt I couldn't see Hedy anymore. It wouldn't be good for my relationship with his second wife. It wouldn't have mattered to my son if Hedy remained my friend, but I couldn't handle an 'ex' and an 'in' at the same time."

Some of you, of course, never loved your in-law child and, in fact, experience relief at his exit from the family. You are glad your child is "over" that one. Maybe you feel he or she married too young, or originally felt it was the wrong mate. You might have preferred an in-law child whose background was more like yours, or just felt your child was unhappy. These are some reasons parents have given us for feeling content about the divorce. If your story fits this pattern, you will have little trouble letting go of your in-law child.

When there are grandchildren, more is at stake. The relationship between you and your ex-law is larger than the question of regret over her loss. She may have custody of, and prime influence over, "the future of your family," with little input from you. The fear of losing contact with your grandchildren could prompt you to keep in as close touch as possible. If she blames you for the trouble in the marriage or just never liked you, she can withhold those children entirely or carefully ration your time with them. The struggle between you may once have been covert and polite. You can now expect an outright vindictive battle unless she tolerates you in hopes of your financial contribution to their support. Your grandchildren could be the pawns in a horrible power struggle.

A grown grandchild still shudders as she tells us:

> My grandmother would come to the door of our apartment. She wanted to see my sister and me. She would ring the bell. Mom wouldn't answer. Then Grandma would go to the lobby and make a scene. She'd ring the super's bell or call us on the phone. One time my mother went to the lobby and hit her. We were so embarrassed. I was only five. . . . When I look back, I don't think I cared about anybody then. I didn't side with my mother, nor was I interested in my grandparents' coming to visit. I can't even remember caring about the divorce. I just wanted the turmoil to go away. That was all that mattered.

Of course, that grandmother aggravated her grandchild's stress. There are other ways to handle frustration besides scenes in the lobby. Fortunately, today there are legal avenues to open up visiting rights if they are denied you.

If your daughter has given custody to your son-in-law, you are probably very angry with her. You may respond by pitching in to help him as much as you can, but he may not continue to want your help. When he remarries, there can be trouble. At that time, he may want nothing to do with your family, and you may be shut out from seeing your grandchildren. Wife number two doesn't want you hanging around. If the grandchildren are old enough, you can hope they will insist on seeing you.

Siblings Hanging In

Your other children are not immune to the tremors that run through the mobile. They have some of the sensitivity and confusion that you have. Can the ex-law still be their friend? Where do they stand in the hierarchy of your attention? One mother especially needed her daughter when divorce struck. "I leaned on my daughter Judy a lot. I couldn't comprehend what happened between my son and his wife. They once seemed so happy. Judy was close to her brother. I thought she understood and could help me, and she did." In many cases, it is the brothers and sisters who don't understand the reasons for the divorce and who look to you, the parents, for answers. Some of your children may grow guarded and judgmental, constantly watching that you don't give too much money to the divorcer or some furniture that they may covet. Others may move away from you, physically and emotionally, since you are concentrating on the divorcer.

"When I look back on my own marriage," says one brother of a divorcer, "I think it improved after Rick and Barbara split up. Rick moved home to Mom and Dad, and I think I was relieved that he was taking my place as the responsible son. My wife and I got a lot closer, just because I stopped spending every Sunday with my family. I never knew how much she resented that, but now we treasure the day together."

You may find your attitude toward the mates of your other children wavering for a while. You may suddenly be suspicious of other possible separations. Your other children don't understand your guardedness and seemingly unusual questions, and they may resent your changed attitude. You may not even be aware of what is motivating you—that you are scared of another divorce. You and they will get through this murky period. Your divorce anxiety will abate, and your distrust will lessen as your family gets accustomed to the realities and your divorcer stands more firmly on his own feet.

Everybody's Hung up for a While

Many other relationships among family members are stirred by divorce. Your parents will want to know why and how, and can be deeply affected. Your own brothers and sisters, aunts and uncles to your beleaguered child, will have their say. You will feel it at big family celebrations by who gets invited and who is seated next to whom. Divorce is truly the shake-up of the entire family.

The lopsided mobile, which represents the new distance or closeness between you and yours and the way you all hang together, in no way measures the intensity of anger you experience when your own parent accuses you of interfering with your child's marriage. Just as deep is the pleasure you feel when your brother writes an understanding letter or makes a thoughtful offer to your divorcer: "Come with Aunt Janet and me on our next trip," or, "Would you like to have our old car, we're buying a new one?"

The In-Law's Parents

Your in-law's parents may or may not be part of your family mobile, but they certainly shake, too. The main bond between you and them is the tie with your respective children. During the marriage, you may have been allies or just tolerated each other at family get-togethers. Whatever the relationship was, it dwindles with divorce. Those who did not like each other will have a quick parting of ways. You may think "the other side" interfered too much or could have done more for the couple. They may feel that if your child didn't know she could go home to Mama when she was unhappy, the pair might have worked it out. If the parents on both sides were friendly, you may commiserate with each other: "What can we do?" "What do you think?" It is rare that the friendship survives the divorce, though you may feel no enmity to each other.

If there are grandchildren, some delicate rivalrous undercurrents will be more apparent after the divorce. You may resent that the other grandparents buy too many toys; they may think you are stingy and unfeeling if your gift to your grandchild is "only a book." Grandchildren's birthday parties can become

skirmish grounds for grandparents. If you are on the noncustodial side and don't see your grandchildren very often, the
occasion for cakes, candles, and paper hats may seem trying.
Sometimes you are not invited at all, and you feel cheated yet
again.

So many actions that were "givens" suddenly require premed-
itation and planning. The mobile that used to move about
serenely with passing air currents now droops out of kilter. You
are baffled. Your in-law child is no longer part of it; your own
child is in turmoil; and the fate of your grandchildren, your link
to the future, is on hold.

4

The First Months Are the Worst

"Jim moved out! We've split!" These jolting words sound the alarm inside you as loudly as the internal echo of your daughter's screams in the backyard long ago that brought you swooping to the rescue. This shocking news might be in the second paragraph of a perfectly ordinary-looking letter like the one that arrives from Phoenix every week, or you could answer the doorbell and find the whole sorry-looking crew right there—daughter, toddler, and the baby, bearing only a box of disposable diapers, a teddy bear, and a stroller.

When your child rushes from the horrors of a failed relationship, the sole strategy is to get away fast. Some who want out take their toothbrush to the familiar apartment of "the other person," the one who was a catalyst in the breakup. Some flee to friends' homes temporarily or to a hotel. In our version of the story, your child brings it all home to you.

You automatically apply the basic canons of first aid, well known to you from years of drill: heat up some soup and put everyone to bed. You'll cry later.

Whenever we receive shocking news, most of us react violently, inside or out, or both. You are no exception. You probably feel that a whole little pocket of dependability, your child's marriage, has exploded in your face, whether you suspected that your daughter and her husband were having problems or felt that it was a pretty solid marriage. You are numb in these first awful moments and hoping for reconciliation, a chance that they will patch it up. You tell yourself that this latest spat is just a brush fire, that one parent will say the magic words, "I'm sorry," and the stroller, teddy bear, and box of diapers will be trotted home. But you're not convinced of this.

While the "Mom, Dad, I need you" is still a fresh SOS, the kind you haven't heard quite the same way since the marriage began, you recognize that you are not only responding to an emergency but are in a crisis state yourself. This particular chaos seems to have a finality about it—the death of the marriage. During the next three months or so you may not be able to discern which of the many is the most overwhelming anguish. Is it the tremendous fear that your child is not strong enough to withstand the psychological damage of divorce, the division of the property, child custody, and the return to the competitive life of a single? Is it your regret for deeds undone and words spoken or unspoken? Your own mea culpas?

You think, too, about how your spouse will hold up. Will the strain prove too much for a stomach that tends to ulcers or a heart that is weak? Is there the possibility of a major fight between you, each blaming the other for the failure? How will you break the news to your parents, to your brothers and sisters, to your other children? What will your friends think?

How Did They Come to This?

On the lips of every shocked parent are also the questions, "Why? What happened?" You may have a hunch about the whys, or you may be totally in the dark. Whatever your state of mind, this is not the time to plague your child with probing questions. She may want to talk, but she probably won't understand the causes of the split herself, let alone be able to explain it to you and yours. Some day it may add up for you all; often it doesn't.

Fights and the end of the relationship can sometimes be laid at the feet of a power struggle between the couple, each of whom had to have the first and last word. By now their words are so loaded with anger that every exchange is hurtful. Either they believe divorce will relieve their pain, or they figure they have only one life to live and they don't intend to live forever in combat. This is the Second Chance Theory—"I can do better next time."

Perhaps these divorcers never worked out the division of responsibilities—who does what, inside or outside the home. The ongoing struggle for women's rights has led to a blurring of clear marital roles for both men and women. There are no longer traditional duties. Every responsibility has to be discussed and agreed upon. Husbands are expected to share home chores; wives, money-making. The arrival of the first child redirects the focus of the young couple just as it did for you, but with a difference. Who of you fathers had to stay home with the baby because your wife had an important case to try? How many of you mothers took your baby to the daycare center where he has lived all day, every weekday, since he was six weeks old?

Besides juggling crazy work schedules, your children, men and women both, want fulfillment in other areas of their lives. They value play as much as the work ethic and they want it all now. They fill every waking hour, working, jogging, studying for a graduate degree, manning a community hotline. Every day is a pressure cooker and there is no time to cultivate their relationship. Some couples find time for each other and survive, others don't.

Perhaps your son is going through a midlife crisis and is pursuing another woman, in hopes of avoiding or delaying the inevitable. For your daughter there are age-related crises, too. She may be heading toward age forty, worried that she hasn't quite made it in the Big World, or that she isn't pregnant and may never have a baby, or that no man will ever look at her quite that way again.

There are other common factors that propel over-forty couples into divorce. Some have long-standing, low-key dissension, disenchantment, or boredom, or cannot survive the empty nest, the loss of a job, or the death of their own child. Some stressful life event blows their fragile bond to bits. Many marriages break up because one partner outgrew the other. They were both kids when they got married, and then one of them broadened his or her horizon. One script is that the husband moved up in his job to a position where he wanted a more sophisticated or worldly woman by his side. Another version: the wife, fed up with checking "housewife" on all the standard forms, decided to get her college degree. It used to be that college was where a woman got her "Mrs." but nowadays the continuing education department can be a passage to the single life. The housewife begins to think of herself as a potential lawyer, business person, or writer, and a discordant note enters that harmonious marriage. Such a woman often seeks marital (and individual) counseling, and sometimes her husband can be helped to grow alongside her, but if they cannot compose a new basis for harmony, that's the end of that marriage.

Divorce is now occurring in all groups and classes of society, partly because it's not as difficult for women to be alone as it once was. Your separated daughter can now comfortably enter a restaurant by herself and not be ignored. She can obtain a mortgage. She can receive a tax credit for child care while she is at work. She may not yet match the earnings of her male counterpart, but at least it is possible for her to pay the rent, uncork a bottle of domestic wine, and live life comfortably as a divorced woman. Her remarriage future is good, since two-thirds of all divorced women remarry within three years after divorce.

The record for men is even better, since three-quarters of all men remarry in those same three years, usually to a woman who has also been divorced. Big industry, banks, and insurance companies, which formerly discriminated against divorced men, now give them equal billing with family men.

In his own home a divorced man surrounds himself with all

the comforts he had when he was married. He cooks dinners for one, two, or six, sprays his plants, and uses the washer and dryer with ease.

There's a whole big singles' world out there!

What Can You Do Now?

Meanwhile, back at the front door, there is a job to be done. Take your cue from your turbulent grown child. You have to be the calm one. (1) After the soup, see if she needs money. All contributions are welcome. (2) Look to the little ones. They are shattered, too, afraid to be separated from Mommy. The violent outbursts they heard and felt make it seem that their parents might disappear in a cloud of smoke. You represent the stable force to their little eyes, the route to equilibrium. They are accustomed to your ways. Arthur Kornhaber, M.D., co-author of *Grandparents/Grandchildren, the Vital Connection,* says, ". . . the bond between grandparents and grandchildren is second in emotional power and influence only to the relationship between children and parents." "Second" is a comfortable runner-up position.

"Mommy" needs your comfort, too. The first words you utter and your first physical response send signals that your child will well remember through the divorce process. They are important and long-lived. She will immediately sense warmth and acceptance or be put off by what she perceives as coolness or disapproval. If you face the news of the separation as horrifying and degrading, it will show, and you will compound the sense of failure that is surely lurking under her anger and panic. Your job is to provide a tough backstop of support, saving the tsk-tsks for your spouse or confidant. Don't attack your child's spouse. She may, after all, go back to him. Blame no one. The baby words that soothed the five-year-old when she came running and unhappy won't work now, either. You can't offer to whack your in-law child with an umbrella. This time there is an internal wound and you can't make it better by making her laugh. She cannot.

We do not mean to neglect the agony that husbands suffer in the divorce debacle. Your son could be the one who rings the bell, the phone, or writes the explosive letter. He needs the same solace and support. His concerns may be different from a daughter's, yet your son suffers the same sense of failure, loss, and confusion. He may face having custody of the children by choice or default, and that responsibility has its terrors for either parent. He worries, too, that he will lose the children altogether and that they might be angry and blame him for the breakup. He cringes at the idea of another man in his house, acting father to his children. He may have to face alimony and child support and maintain two homes. His life has slid downhill. He wants a second chance and fears he won't be able to afford it.

Son or daughter, both are scared, angry, vulnerable, and fearful of the future. In every stress scale of human experience, the death of a spouse hits the highest number, but separation and divorce are close behind. Respond to the tension of this moment. Let him or her know you are one hundred percent supportive.

Don't be surprised at bizarre behavior on the part of each member of the uncouple. Also, don't panic if your recently separated child straight-arms you or tells you the news in off-hand fashion after the entire world seems to know. Although he cannot yet share his distress with you, your son might tell the whole unpleasant story to someone at work, since strangers will react less intimately. Although your daughter might "dump" on others, she may maintain an icy silence with you. Her reaction, which you translate as rejection, may be because your pain, along with hers, is far too much for her to handle just yet. It can be interpreted as a clear sign that she is certain of your loyalty and love, that you are so close you need no explanations.

Some Things You Can Expect

There are some studies by Levinger and Moles, *Divorce and Separation*, 1979, that offer ways to predict divorce: (1) If your child and his wife continue to share the same house during the separation, they are less likely to finalize it. (2) Another tie that binds is when the husband has a reasonable income, his wife none. That tends to keep the marriage together.

The same team reports the ambivalence of those who are recently separated. Your daughter may be angry or guilty for having contributed to the breakup. She may be awaiting the possibility of her husband's return with both dread and expectation, and be restless, fearful, and in panic at the prospect of a new and different life. Your son-in-law may not sleep or eat well, or he could be euphoric and see the new life ahead as an adventure. Through this whole confused period they may sleep together to combat their loneliness.

We're in This Together

While you are helping or waiting for signals, the stage is full of other action. There is the matter of your spouse. How do you two usually handle big trouble? When your teenage daughter rolled in at two in the morning, high on pot or beer, did you rage at each other for permitting her such freedom, or did you tackle it as a team? You know your own patterns for confronting calamities. Try to respond together with the best supportive action you can muster. Strife between you will only add to the general misery.

If you are the one who has to break the news to your spouse, think over the words you will use. All you know is that your marrieds have separated and your child is shaken. Don't embellish the story or make it more dramatic than it is. When parents battle over the difficulties of their children, their own marriage can suffer and be threatened. If you permit this breakup to rock your own marriage, your child may remarry and be expecting a child—your grandchild—before your own divorce papers are signed.

Some couples blame each other for any perceived weakness in their children, ranging from report-card failure to what the family sees as disgrace: divorce. Those who find it necessary to fix blame on others are trying to absolve themselves. All errors for them are someone else's fault. Others flog themselves because they failed to baby-sit last Sunday or refused to lend money for the mortgage. They believe these actions were the crucial pin in the marriage and contributed to the separation. And finally, there are parents who experience great disappointment. They were happy with the marriage. The familiar progression of their child's family carrying on beyond them has been stopped in its tracks. Their proud entrance into family parties with grown child, in-law child, and possibly grandchildren is over. They now feel belittled, diminished, failed.

It could be helpful if husband and wife air each individual fear and look at it. It's easier that way, and the trouble does not seem so enormous.

The Blues and the Dumps

If what scares you most is the depressed feeling you have that doesn't seem to go away, there are things to do that can help you. You can talk to the people who will understand your feelings: your spouse, friends, and family. Talking to other parents who are in the throes of a child's separation or have gone through a child's divorce is a good idea, too.

The biggest boost is to tackle your concerns one at a time, one day at a time. Don't think *divorce*, think *di-vor-ce*, a little at a time. Don't feel depressed about being depressed. You are suffering a loss.

Remember that the divorce process is not forever. Your child will get another chance. As for you, think of your past losses: parents, relatives, friends. Time really is the great healer.

If your blues interfere with your life, you might want to consider counseling. One route is pastoral guidance. Religious leaders are called more frequently to help with troubled marriages than for any other reason. Many members of the clergy have taken courses in this field and learned the skills that enable them to hear you effectively and give counsel. The soaring divorce rate has produced lots of marriage and divorce counselors. Social workers, psychologists, and psychiatrists have practices devoted to these problems. Some are affiliated with centers. Some are private practitioners. When you derive benefit from counseling, you can be more helpful to your child. He might even decide to follow your example and get some help himself if he sees that it works for you. If you are hide-bound by the old stereotype of "the couch," be assured that there is very little likelihood that you will have to dredge up your memory of your hateful baby brother in these sessions. You may only need a few visits, in which specific suggestions can help you see new ways to handle your uneasiness.

"I" After "We" Is a Lonely Word

You sense the loneliness in your child immediately. So much energy was directed to escaping the bad marriage that she ran headlong, never considering what life alone would be like. Living in a hotel room is vacuous; crowding in with friends begins to pall. Even your home, in the same old room, is no comfort and often gives your child a sense of going backward. During the first three months, the emptiness may force your daughter to contemplate a return to the marriage, or at least to wait a while before calling a lawyer and saying the fateful words, "I want a divorce." Your son will feel let down and adrift. Everything seems temporary, and "we" has become "I," a lonely word. A separated person is on hold. The finality he will feel when the divorce master stamps the petition "divorce granted" closes that chapter. He now believes that the worst is over.

During the separation period your child will act out, shout out, sleep out, even pig out. Your daughter may come home at two in the morning and rise at seven to get to her office. If your son responds to every phone invitation to join a party, he is probably reassuring himself that someone still thinks he is attractive. They are seeking a sense of wholeness.

Yet, your child could withdraw. She could retreat from family, friends, and maybe from work. There seems to be nothing you can do to relieve the suffering. Offers of a paid vacation may give brief relief, but his or her depression is real, and he or she has to go through the process of mourning the loss. Grief cannot be rushed, but it is usually self-limiting.

You Are Not Number One

You are often the targets for the anger that accompanies depression. Your son may smash your print of his wedding picture or the cheese board he and his wife gave you for your anniversary. An innocent question can spark resentment. "How did things go at work today?" can be met with a defensive, "Fine!" as though your daughter thinks you expected her day to have been terrible.

Don't expect your child even to think about how all this is affecting you. A marriage counselor we interviewed said, "When the divorcing couple comes in and we start to talk about parents, neither of them ever mentions Mom's or Dad's pain. I think part of that might be that couples who do come to us tend to be totally focused on themselves, not even on their kids. They can't get out of their skin emotionally to acknowledge that anyone else exists."

Healing

The strength and personality of your child affects the depth of your concern over whether he will successfully break out of his gloom and anger and be able to trust and love again. If your daughter was always a fighter and handled well what came down the pike, you are pretty sure she will deal with this crisis, too. If your son's childhood was full of tears and despair, you may worry. Remember that both children, battler and weeper, grew to adulthood and married. That is certainly survival. Besides, weepers often grow up to be battlers. Don't prejudge.

While you still ache with your child's pain and your own, you may notice that the heavy pall of the first months is lifting and a healing process has begun. You laugh together and now and then you detect references to a new "friend" in his conversation. If your son buys a new suit or your daughter new makeup, you feel encouraged. You are able to talk about the separation more easily with your family and friends. You even let yourself think about another wedding and the possible grandchildren it may bring. Hope springs, and you settle into the business of acceptance on the road to normalcy.

5

Whose Side Are You On?

Whenever we run into Bill, my ex, and it seems to happen almost too often for it to be an accident, my parents make a fuss over him, hug him, invite him to visit them; and even though we have been divorced for a year and a half, I stand far away from that little reunion. I feel they are plotting to get us back together, and that they like him better than they like me. They always did! He seems to have, in their eyes, all the qualities they think I don't.

—MARCI

Ever since Marci's divorce, we can't do anything right. She accuses us of not loving her, but that's ridiculous. It's true we loved Bill, and we still haven't gotten over that he's not one of our children. But we've taken his name out of our will, we've stopped inviting him to family occasions, what more can we do? We can't pretend we never knew him.

—MARCI'S PARENTS

My Family Right or Wrong

Divorce is a battle and you can't avoid the reality of taking sides. You can say it's *their* fight, not yours, and try to stay uninvolved (you can't). You can insist that your child must be in the right (maybe yes, maybe no). You can say, "Let's be fair, wait and see until we know the whole story." (*Fair* is a word for weather forecasters and umpires.)

> We always liked to be fair. When Tom said he was leaving Alison we couldn't believe it. He "outgrew" her? What does that mean? She was a perfect wife and daughter-in-law. She adored him, did everything for him. She was good to us, too. We were never sure he appreciated her, treated her right. We told him that when he told us about the divorce. It has been three years. We hear from Alison, but not from our son, not on holidays, not on birthdays. He has given us up. It's as though he were dead. What did we do that was so terrible?

The old adage, "My family, right or wrong," is an absolute during this rickety time. You may be tormented by questions, such as, "How shall I treat my daughter-in-law? I love her! Should I call my son-in-law? Can I send a birthday card? Is it right to call the other family? Should I know the other side?" The answer to all these questions is that your child has to be Number One with you. All contacts and arrangements with your ex-law must be made with your child's knowledge and consent. If you try to go around him—like Tom's parents in our story—you will be tempting his anger and possible estrangement. This is not the time to say, "on the one hand, but on the other hand," nor to call your in-law-to-be-ex-law in secret to ask if you can help. Now is the time to put that more recent addition to your family on a back burner and to focus on your child.

Be aware that there are two stages in being loyal to your child after separation: (1) the first months, and (2) when things are calmer. During those first, hardest months it is best to support the side of your child, even though you know there's another side. This is not only for the sake of your child but also for the preservation of your family. It stands to reason that you remain on the side of your child both at the altar for the wedding and for the separation and divorce. Most of the parents we talked to feel that this rock-bottom allegiance between parent and child is what family is all about, but some—like Marci's parents and Tom's—find it hard to carry out.

Your child will be sensitive to your response and pick up clues before they are out of your mouth. "How could you do this to us?" translates into your greater concern about saving your face than your daughter's. If you say to your son, "How could you do this to Ginny and the children?" you are displaying loyalty to the in-law and grandchildren, not to him. If you are going to back up your child to the finish, let him know you are there. Save the painful questions for a later and less threatening time. Respond to the questions of family and friends with only the barest details of what you know about the divorce. Don't throw yourself into the role of critic. To your child, that feels like disloyalty too. Be a supportive good friend. You may not get thank-you's right off, but be patient, the rewards will come.

There is a quid pro quo for backing up your child. You hope for some openness from her, and perhaps for an unnegotiated, tacit promise to stand behind you when you are in need. What you want in return is something you don't talk about much, not to your child or friends or relatives. The words *duty* and *filial* responsibility come harder to you than they did to your parents. Yet, as you move into middle age, you say to each other, "Who will take care of us when we need it? Will we end up in a nursing home when we can't function on our own? Is loyalty really a one-way street?" It is for you right now.

In the midst of all your confusion over the changes in your family mobile, the words are: "My child, right or wrong."

You Are Number One with Us

There are rewards in this loyalty to your child. In the best cases, you and your child will grow closer because of your one hundred percent constancy. One mother said:

All these years, throughout her marriage, Ellie was "at" us. She criticized my clothes, my hair, my meals. She called her father "stuffy." I thought it was going to be like that forever. Now that Ellie and Jack have divorced, I have come to the conclusion that she was so brainwashed by what he kept saying about us that she believed it. We really did not ever like him, and I guess he knew it and hated us. Now she is a totally different person. She seems to think we are okay. We help her out as much as we can and enjoy doing it.

A divorced man confesses:

I have come to see why my parents did not like Joan. She wasn't warm, and she was always criticizing them and I guess she was tough on me, too. They have been there for me through this whole mess. I know now that I didn't like things about her they didn't like, but was afraid to admit that, even to myself.

Even if you continue to love and appreciate your in-law child, the bond between you and your child will strengthen because of your solid support. Your son will be grateful for your consideration of his needs in this lonely time. He may not always express it. Often that gratitude shows in indirect fashion. One father said: "Mark and I have long talks now that he is single again. I have let out my feelings. I don't think I ever talked to him or anyone in just this way before. We get together as two men in a different way than we ever did."

You may talk more openly "man to man" or "man to Mom" because, in a sense, you are all in this together. If your son is suffering feelings of abandonment, your backup is a lifeline. You set an extra place at the table "just in case." Your life takes on new meaning, a comfortable déjà vu. It is like those days of his childhood when he stayed too late at the ball game and showed up late for dinner. You were so glad he was home at last that you forgot to be angry.

You will take great joy in watching your grandchild and your

daughter enjoying each other, a sort of "two against the world."
One grandmother said, "Since Alan left, Jonel is teaching Alex
to knit. They take long walks together and talk to each other
about school, friends, and plans over dinner."

Caution! The parent-child relationship you are observing
may not resemble that rosy picture. You may see your child too
sad and self-absorbed to be patient with your grandchild or
misdirecting to your grandson the anger meant for her husband.
You may see your granddaughter act fresh or misbehave because
she blames her mother (your daughter) for the divorce. These
situations may tax your patience, but this is the time when your
sad child or angry grandchild needs your support and understanding.

There are other cautions as well. Sometimes your child will
make it difficult to back her up. She may be angry or afraid of
her need to depend on you again or grieving too deeply to
respond. "My child hates me!" cried one mother. "I want to
help Bill but he evades me," complained a father. It is hard to
remain steadfast when you feel rejected and misunderstood.
This does not mean you should maintain a relationship with
your ex-law, for this will be construed as siding with him. Like
Marci, at the beginning of this chapter, seeing her parents
embrace her ex-law at parties only confirmed her fears that they
were against her.

Another common test of loyalty occurs when you feel your
child has acted badly and is to blame for the divorce. This is a
frequent accusation when there are grandchildren and your
child has had an affair. On the surface, it appears clear-cut
who's at fault, but reserve judgment. Your child may have been
provoked or had good reason to seek satisfaction outside the
marriage. If you hear him out and still disagree, you may have a
difficult choice.

A grandmother tells of her decision:

> I gave my son a lot of leeway. I listened to what he had to say
> about Fran and I could see she was always nagging and complain-

ing, but I didn't think this gave him the right to introduce one of his kids to his girlfriend. After the separation he moved into her apartment, and I didn't like that either. I thought he was being selfish and then he got fooling around with the alimony and child support and it was very bad for the kids, so even though he didn't want me to contact Fran, I finally decided, "Which is better for the grandchildren?" I felt I had to choose between my son and my grandchildren, and I was disgusted with him.

When your grandchildren are being victimized by your child's actions, your best course might be to concern yourself with their needs and wait and hope that their father or mother will come around.

Grandparents on the noncustodial side of the family sometimes report a kind of disastrous fallout from the explosion. For instance: "Our son was at our house when his wife came to see him. They had a fight and right then and there she decided she'd pay him back by not letting us see the grandchildren." This can happen whether or not you actively back up your child. During the first white heat of separation, your ex-law may see anyone connected with her husband as "poison to the children." Usually the heat will subside in time, and with it the venom. Meanwhile, get your message to your daughter-in-law that you respect her rights and privileges as a parent, but that your prime concern is your grandchildren, for whom you feel a fierce love and loyalty.

He's in the Air, You're on the Ground

While your son is banking on your loyal safety net, and even contemplating a new life for himself, you may be mourning the absence of your daughter-in-law. Way back when he chose his wife, you liked her, and you would surely love her now if you could. She was "family." You enjoyed listening to her plans. You liked the way she looked at your son. She gave you warm responses. It felt like love. If you were a second-string parent to your in-law child, it is hard suddenly to become the enemy. You are still attached to the past, while your child is busy detaching himself from it. Don't think you and your son can look at the breakup with such different eyes without disappointing each other many times.

> SON: I've met this great girl. I'd like to show her off to my parents. They don't seem anxious to meet my dates. They still hope Julie and I will kiss and make up. No way!

> MOTHER: I don't know why Jim thinks I want to meet his girlfriends. It upsets me to see him with someone else. We loved Julie and I miss her. I need more time.

He is ready for his next romance, you are not, nor were lots of the parents with whom we conferred, especially during the first year.

This is a period of transition. Change is full of chaos and turmoil. Understanding what your child is going through can help you handle her irritability, her straight-arming you at times, but you are hurting too. Don't feel guilty about your own mixed responses. Although you may have no hesitancy about backing up your child, you may have a lot of uncertainty about losing your ex-law. The truth is that many parents we interviewed expressed regret. This father's daughter had divorced the man who was the son he never had:

> We meet for lunch at this bar. We talk about football and fishing over beer and sandwiches, like we used to. I never thought I'd miss him so much. I don't tell my wife or my daughter. They wouldn't understand. What they don't know won't hurt them, and we honestly never talk about them or the divorce.

If that divorcee heard about these meetings she would be furious and think her father was meddling; but her father had his pain and loss to handle and did so as best he could.

If your daughter left the mate you felt was right for her, you may be angry at her. If you look on the divorce as yet another failure for her, she will know it, spoken or not, and pull away. If you criticize the way your son is going about his divorce, he will be infuriated. You may have your angers, too. You felt that your child was settled, two by two, and that the couple took care of each other. You may resent having to take on renewed responsibility for a child you thought was married off. You like the post-childrearing freedom of your life. This new plea for help seems like an intrusion. These reactions on your part are legitimate and common.

You and your child may not rush into each other's arms when the news of the separation erupts. "I always really and truly was on my daughter-in-law's side," admitted one mother soon after the separation. "My son did things I felt were outrageous, and I said so. I am just that kind of person. I didn't stick with him because he was my son. But now she looks at me the way she looks at him, with fury and hostility. We're one and the same to her. I guess I understand that, but it hurts." You and your child could be at standoff positions, both of you suffering shock. If you, the parents, offer real backup and no backtracking in spite of your feelings, the linkage between you will be forged, or reforged, to help you, your child, and your family survive the trauma. You are in it together for sure.

One fact that must not be overlooked is that many parents don't want to see their ex-law at all. When asked when she planned to see her ex-law child, one mother snapped, "Never, thank God!" You, too, may not have liked your daughter-in-law; or you may feel too guilty about seeing your ex-son-in-law. If you are glad that he or she is out of your life, that's fine. It could be the best way to handle a severed relationship.

To resume the metaphor of the family mobile, you must not forget that your parents are part of the balance, too. Their loyalty is an easy one for them. For the most part, there is no doubt in their minds. They *know* that the baby they were permitted to diaper and babysit for, now grown, can do no wrong. They lay all the blame on the ex-law, to whom they have little attachment. "She was never good enough for him" is the way they justify the breakup. They don't want to hear that their practically perfect grandson was not the perfect mate. They know that "my family, right or wrong" means "my family is always right."

Second Stage Loyalty

Remember, divorce is a process. Put your ex-law child out of your orbit until the period of acrimony between the divorcers passes. Then, when there is rational behavior between the couple again and angers are cooled, you may want to let out tentative feelers, hoping he or she will accept them. This is stage two. There is no way to predict when that moment will arrive, but you will know it in your child's changed attitude toward the whole messy business.

One mother reported that, after the divorce was final, her son's anger seemed banked and she called her ex-law. They met occasionally for some good heart-to-hearts. "It made me feel better to talk to her, let her know I didn't blame her. She told me she was doing all right. Now I can sleep at night without rehearsing how I might tell her how sorry I am." There is no rule that dictates hatred for an ex-law. You might be glad to see each other through the years.

Talk it over with your child before you leap into such a reunion. Rage can smolder for a long time, as this couple discovered:

We stayed in touch with Janet for many years because of the grandchildren. We never thought our son Bill cared. We took it for granted he understood, and he never said anything. Then his oldest daughter got married. Just before the wedding he called us up, enraged. "I don't want you sitting at the head table with Janet and her family," he said. He and his second wife were seated at another table and he let us know what he expected of us. He staked his claim and we were very surprised.

Like the son of this couple, your child may hold his feelings inside for a long time. You cannot assume he is neutral. He may harbor his sense of your lack of loyalty for many years.

One seventy-three-year-old woman told us that her son, who had always called her daily, stopped talking to her altogether because she had lunch with his ex-wife. The son was remarried and his current wife was insulted, feeling she had never been accepted as the new daughter-in-law. It was hard for the older woman to understand the rift. She loved both daughters-in-law and she was a lonely widow. If she had discussed the luncheon first with her son, they might have developed an understanding. As it was, the son felt betrayed and his second wife felt rejected.

How Will We See the Grandchildren?

In all this consideration of loyalty, you have to examine your relationship with your grandchildren. You are so important to one another. The situation differs depending on whether your child or your ex-law has custody. Your connection with your ex-law can affect how and when you see those grandchildren. Most grandparents on the noncustodial side report that they go to their ex-law with some sort of conciliatory gesture following the separation. "If there's anything we can do to give you a hand, you know you can count on us," is a typical offer. Those grandparents feel that it is in the best interests of the kids for them to reach out that way. Those confused grandchildren need them, especially after going through their parents' divorce. If it means tact or compromise, it is well worth it.

Your ex-law may have misgivings, as this one did: "When I first told Joe's parents we were going to be separated, his mother came to reassure me that she wanted to maintain contact. Now I take that with a grain of salt, and I think I did even then because I saw the ulterior motive. She really wanted to make sure that she saw her grandchildren, and I resent her for that." There is no question that you have an ulterior motive in wanting to see your grandchildren, but there is also no question that when their parents' divorce occurs, grandchildren like to feel that they can count on you.

A caution! When you are with your grandchildren, don't overplay your position of absolute loyalty. Their antennae are always up. Your ex-law child is, after all, their mother or father. Keep your judgments to yourself. You can *ask* about the ex-law, but don't *talk* about her. Many children we talked to knew their grandparents did not like their mother, but did not care as long as they did not have to take sides.

We heard many unhappy tales from grandparents, of alienation between them and their grandchildren. You could have to face anger from these storm-tossed children. Their mother could keep up the theme of how you "meddled" or that the divorce was your fault. One distraught grandmother wailed: "It's the saddest thing in my life. John and Abby keep saying, 'You made our dad leave our mom.' I try to explain that it is hard to lay blame in a divorce. I only see them when they are with my son. They don't run to me when I visit. They hardly ever hug or kiss me. I am alone, a widow. I need them and I think they need me, so I keep trying." Since we spoke with her initially that grandmother feels she is making some progress. Time is slowly healing the rift. She invites her grandchildren to visit her one at a time. Grandma lives in Philadelphia, and she and John love exploring the Franklin Institute together. When Abby comes, they swim and cook together.

Don't ask your grandchildren lots of questions about their lives with their "other parent." They have their sensibilities and loyalties to handle. An "other parent" complained, "Every time my children visit Jed's parents, they feel as though they are being grilled for information. They come home nervous and upset and it is several days before they calm down from a visit."

On the other hand, this grandfather was surprised at the sophistication of his grandchildren: "They know when they are with us they don't talk about their father's family. 'How's your dad? He's fine.' They instinctively protect themselves. It's amazing!"

And So Do His Sisters . . .

Don't forget your other children in this period of loyalty. They have their sensitivities too. They may feel neglected if you focus too much on the one in the throes of divorce, as this brother did: "They can't talk about anything but Louise and her child these days. My sister's a grown woman and partly responsible for what happened. She'll handle it and she should. She's perfectly capable. You'd think she was an infant!"

Make time to talk it over with your other children, as Mrs. S. did: "I had to talk to Linda because she was being very narrow-minded about her sister Ellen's divorce. Linda's husband was dying and she couldn't understand why anyone would voluntarily end a marriage." Mrs. S. reminded Linda of how unhappy Ellen had been for several years and what a much more immature man Ellen's husband was than Linda's. In this way she kept the two sisters from growing more apart at a time when both of them needed each other and her more than ever.

It is quite possible that your other children will have a tough time separating out their loyalties. If they felt a close friendship with the ex-law and loved him, it is hard for them to give him up. We heard this over and over again. Sometimes they continue to see him quietly, to listen to "the other side." If they feel close, they will try doubly hard to figure out the best way to handle the changed relationship. "I love Charlie as a brother," explained one woman. "We were friends before the marriage and I don't want to give him up just because Sallie wants out!"

Talking together as a family can help you all sort out who is what to whom. Some families we saw try to find more time together to provide a web of support for the divorcer. In the middle of a Thanksgiving dinner, one family began a shouting match about loyalty and whether the ex-daughter-in-law should have been invited. The separation was only a month old. The eldest son exploded, "You're acting as though nothing happened! My brother was pushed out of his own home. The least you can do is stand solidly with him. Forget about her and her feelings!" That outburst helped everyone argue it out and decide that their loyalties lay with their own family member.

And His Cousins and His Aunts

Mother-in-law: "Doris, we will pick the boys up tomorrow. Put on their good suits. We're all going to cousin Frank's wedding."

That recently separated daughter-in-law, now living with her parents, had thought her in-laws liked her and that they resented her husband's leaving her and the two boys. She still felt part of his family. The phone call was a shocker. Doris had expected that she, too, would have been invited to a family wedding, since she was still a member of the family. It was fear of an awkward situation that prompted Doris's in-laws to exclude her, and through this rejection they risked their continuing relationship with their grandchildren.

If there is a wedding or any other family occasion coming up, you might discuss with the appropriate family members their invitation plans for the divorced part of the family. Being included or not can have a long-lasting effect on family relationships and can say as much as an exchange of four-letter words. In some instances we learned of aunts and uncles who continued to invite the ex-law to celebrations because they liked the ex- or because they felt "once in the family, always in the family," but this is always at the risk of offending the blood relative, unless he has given his consent.

Divorce is a time of uncertainty for your aunts, uncles, and cousins, and, though you may be busy with your own concerns, you can't ignore their reactions. They will have questions: "How did it happen? Who's to blame?" You don't have any obligation to tell them the juicy stories. It is doubtful that you know them anyway. For your part, you probably expect, deep down, that the extended family will side with your child. They usually do.

His and Her Parents

While you are counting how many people are affected by the breakup, don't forget the other family closely involved in the change—your ex-law's parents. During the marriage you probably tried to maintain contact with them "for the sake of the kids" or because you genuinely liked them. Many ethnic groups emphasize the practice of being close to your child's in-laws, to cement the larger family. If you are part of such a group, it can make the break even harder.

If you were good friends with that couple, you're now in a quandary. (1) Should you reflect the fury of your child? Remember, your child's anger is his own. You have to decide if you are the angry one and not reflect your child's wrath. (2) Do you have to respect your child's wishes on this one, too? If you like your ex-law's parents and they like you, a cordial relationship may resume after you all come out of the shock. This is part of second-stage loyalty. However, unless you share the common bond of grandchildren, this relationship between you and the other set of parents tends to peter out of its own accord. (3) Will they feel loyalty to your child? You may be disappointed in them if they vent their distress on her, but that is her problem and one of the prices of divorce she must pay.

In our interviews, grandchildren and which parent has custody seemed to make the real difference in the attitudes of the two sets of parents. One widow lamented, "Our Greek family ties are binding and sacred. Even though our children went through with the divorce against all our wishes, we are still friends, even family. We meet when our grandchildren have special occasions."

What Kind of Friends Are They Anyway?

Beyond kinfolk there are close friends who are important to you. Can you expect them to respect your loyalty? They may have liked your ex-law and would like to continue to see him. Their perception of the divorce probably is totally different from yours. They might want to retain the friendship, but the likelihood is they will not.

"We always liked Pauline and Carl's son-in-law. We played tennis with him and laughed together a lot. It is fun to have friends who are young. We had him to dinner last week and it was strained. He might have been wondering what we might tell his ex-laws about him. Of course, we wouldn't say anything. Then we began to wonder if they might think we would all talk about them when we were together. We wouldn't, of course, but we decided it was better not to call him again, and he hasn't called us either."

Then there are the friends of the couple. They may try to keep the lines open to both members of the divorcing couple, at first. Mostly they establish themselves in one camp or another before long, most frequently the woman's side. That is painful for your son. Don't be critical of these actions, especially to your child. It is an awkward and agonizing situation for their friends to take sides. They hear each one's version of the story from both Dick and Jane. They try not to talk to him about her, or to her about him. They have lost one friend, possibly two. How they respond to their confusion is their choice, not yours. Don't call and suggest they get in touch with your child if they have not. *That is meddling!*

One thoughtful young woman we talked to for several hours described her confusion, postseparation, predivorce: "You were defined so recently in so many ways by so many people as part of a pair, even if it wasn't a wholly happy one, that you feel lost and deserted when it's done with. You are not sure where your friends' loyalties lie. You are on the alert for any signal that lets you know where they stand."

Friends and relatives will move in one direction or another, some continuing their loyal friendship with the husband, some with the wife. While these decisions are signaling stop or go to your child, your loyalty must be unmistakable.

6

Do We Really Mean Come Home?

Welcome to Overtime

If your house has an extra bedroom, if you are reasonably healthy and fairly sound financially, and if you did not cry "shame, shame" when you heard that the marriage might fall apart, your distressed child could fly like a pigeon to the place called home. Where else can the refrigerator be opened without an invitation to "help yourself" or can mail be forwarded—no questions asked. Your son or daughter, just separated, is running from misery. All his or her emotional and physical energy is exerted toward getting away, getting out, but almost no thought has been given to where. This child who arrives seeking refuge is a tangle of anger (at his or her spouse), rejection because love has changed to vicious hate, and failure because he or she has failed marriage.

You can be helpful and so can your other children. The strength of your family gives a sense of stability, of people who continue to love him. Home can be a hospice for healing.

At divorce time your child may regress. If so, when and if he comes home, he tends to see you in your downhome role, especially now. In your work life, you may preside over a board room with ten arm chairs swiveled in your direction, or lead a white-coated parade through hospital halls to surgery, but at home you are just Dad and Mom.

You are being invaded by your homing pigeon, so before you hear about the technicolor fight that seems to have ended the marriage, say your piece. As you help with the bags and boxes, and put an extra blanket on the bed say (in your own words), "I know that as soon as you can, you will want to find your own place!"

As for who can be expected to knock at your door, surprisingly enough, more sons than daughters come home, but for shorter periods. Their wives and children usually remain in the home they all shared, and sons need a place to "crash" until they set themselves up somewhere.* Also, most likely to return to the family fold are sons and daughters in financial need, with small children, those who fear abuse, and those who have never lost their dependence on mother, father, or both.

When we asked people about the separation, divorce, and their child's return home, they spilled over with accounts of how it happened to them.

Three Stories

Mrs. D., mother, fifty-six years old:

Valerie rang the bell at three in the morning, Joey, two months old, in her arms. She had fled from an all-night fight with her husband and knew only to come home. If she had not had the baby, I would have taken her into the kitchen, made tea for us, and told her to calm down and go right back to Rob. Her father and I knew our parents would never have taken us back. We have had to suffer through our fights all these years and stay together to face the next day. Sometimes we didn't talk for a week and living in the same house with him was torture. Well, Valerie had little Joey with her and I couldn't think of turning them away. I never

*Ahrons and Bowman, "Changes in Family Relationships Following Divorce of Adult Child: Grandmothers' Perceptions," *Journal of Divorce*, 1982.

dreamed that baby would still be with me when he was a twenty-year-old college student.

My husband said, "Of course we'll take them in," hugged Valerie, and told her not to worry. But I was the one stuck with a full household again. Two months later, I went back to work to add to our income (to run away?) and insisted that my daughter stay home to mother her baby. Yet, at the end of the day, I made the dinner, I ran the house, and I baby-sat, too, so that Valerie could have a social life. The only help my husband provided was to take Joey on a walk Saturday and Sunday, and on the way they counted the air-conditioners. Rob showed up irregularly and carted our grandson off to the ball game or to some amusement park, always something he wanted, certainly not anything for a toddler. He provided support money now and then, too. Fifteen dollars a week, barely enough to pay for Joey's milk and cookies, was the most he ever contributed.

Valerie and I always got along. When she entered her late teens, I had the feeling that she was my younger sister whom I loved and would always care for. There is no question that I acted emotionally and from a sense of duty when she came home in trouble.

We had a younger daughter at home and having the baby in the house ruined her growing-up years. She was no longer the only child, who could fill the house with teenage friends, but instead she always had to be aware that noise might awaken Joey. Her friends couldn't sing and dance in the living room because the baby's things took up most of the space. As Joey grew older, we always felt that we had to overindulge him and understand him because he was growing up without a father. When Val finally remarried, Joey was fourteen and he refused to leave the only home he'd ever known.

I'm fifty-eight years old now and have a twenty-year-old college student with me. I worry about him when he is out too late, and about drugs and sex. I feel a load of anger at having been trapped. But what else can you say to your daughter, whom you love, when she rings your bell during the night and has her baby in her arms?

Valerie's mother gave an unqualified "yes, come" and lived to regret it. Both father and mother responded as natural parents, opening their home to their daughter, no strings attached. Valerie remained the child she had been when she left home to marry Rob, and when she found a new love, new marriage, left her son behind. Joey obviously chose to remain an overindulged grandchild rather than battle the problems of handling a new father and a new home. Valerie's parents acted emotionally, out of a sense of duty, and found their own later years had been sacrificed, and still after twenty years weren't sure if they would ever live alone together again.

Mr. N., father, sixty-two years old:

Scott was eighteen years old when I handed him two thousand dollars and told him to make his home elsewhere. If I hadn't done this, he would have destroyed my marriage. As soon as his mother and I rescued him from one disaster, he raced around until he found the next one. When we saw his door closed, we knew that he was smoking pot, snorting cocaine, or had sneaked some girl into his room. If we bought a bottle of scotch, it disappeared. Our silver candlesticks, wedding presents from my parents, went too. Each time something happened, I blamed my wife and she blamed me. We were worn out with the terrible problems my son brought to our doorstep and the way he made my wife and me turn on each other. Finally, I told Scott to leave. The money I handed him was a one-time gift and he knew it. Money didn't flow into our household. I'm a carpenter and I work hard for my dollars. My wife might help out in someone's store before Christmas, but she doesn't work outside the home and that's the way I always wanted it to be. She enjoys our home and it always looks nice.

Scott found a small apartment, got a job, and lost it—got another, and lost that one too. He had dinner with us every Sunday and we were glad to see him come and glad to see him go. We knew he was seeing someone steadily, maybe he was living with her, and when we met her they said they were going to be married and she was pregnant. She was heavily into drugs and alcohol. After the first baby, there was a second one, and in between, the neighbors phoned us three times that the police were at his house because they were beating each other up. After one of those brawls, Scott wanted to leave and asked if he and the children could come home to us. I said no because there was no change in him. Instead, I offered to be his landlord, bought a small house, and he pays rent to me. I paid the cost of his divorce, but he still sees his ex-wife. Whenever he can't find a baby-sitter, he can bring the children to my wife, and because of this Scott has been able to keep a steady job as a checker in a supermarket.

The only good thing my son ever did was to father two beautiful babies. They are wonderful grandchildren. I have no regrets about turning him away from our home twice. My wife and I can't figure out why he is the way he is. No one else in our family gave anyone such trouble.

That parent stood firm and never regretted his decision. Apparently, their son could live with it since he continued to come home weekly for dinner and did not deny them the pleasure of his children. Scott's father said, "No, you can't come home, but I'll help."

Mrs. B., mother, forty-seven years old:

When Maryann, my daughter, left her husband, I was proud of her, but I couldn't understand my reaction. After all, I had been divorced, and during the years following my divorce, three of my four children had run away—or just left. I am forty-seven years old and I married at eighteen because I became pregnant while in my freshman year at college. My parents pressured me into marriage and it was a nightmare. My husband beat me, made up to other women in front of me, humiliated me, and constantly criticized the way I cooked and the way I cared for the children. Finally,

I divorced him, but I always felt that I had failed as a wife.

One of my daughters also married at eighteen. She is one of the three who left home. Her husband came from a lower social class than we, and he and his family were all heavy drinkers. He was quick-tempered and pushed her around constantly. They had one child, a son, and when he was six, my daughter walked out of the marriage.

I offered her a month with me until she got on her feet and we grew very close during this time. I saw her become depressed, self-pitying, and angry, and taking out the anger she meant for her husband on her child, just as I had done on mine. I finally understood why my children left my home.

My daughter and I are close friends, and my grandson and I love each other very much. I shared my new insights with my daughter and it has helped her handle her outbursts. Her divorce and her return to my home helped us both. We both gained strength and understanding and wonderful friendship. Three years have gone by and Maryann and my grandson Frank live just down the block. She works and I work, but we make dinner together several times a week and every weekend. Frank, now a nine-year-old Little Leaguer, stays overnight with me. Maryann has some friends, men and women, and I am content with my work, my daughter, and my grandson.

Maryann's mother did not sink into an abyss because she saw her own marriage failure repeated in her daughter's life. Instead, she recognized the familiar signs of displaced anger and self-blame, and together Maryann and her mother sorted out the hurts and found a new relationship. Instead of sinking with the failed marriages, they gained strength together. They shared their misery and their responses and a home for a specific period of time. The experience was healing.

Your "Come Home" Story

If your child reaches out for sanctuary with you and you can and wish to offer it, think in terms of "limits" rather than total sacrifice. The opening of your home to her needs should include your plans for your life as well as hers. Among generations past, the "empty nest" was a time of grief for mothers who had devoted at least twenty years to cooking, baking, washing, and cleaning, to home and school, Cub Scouts, and getting the children to and from parties, and suddenly they had no role. They were bereft, lonely. But today the work force of the United States has 44,190,000 women,* 47.8 percent** of all women. Today's working mother whose child returns home because of marital mishap usually does not breathe that old sigh of relief because baby has come home and life is full again.

Your living pattern slid into a new rhythm when one child or all the children left. The TV might have been moved to your bedroom, winter clothes were transferred to empty closets, and cigarette smoke no longer hung heavy in the draperies. You liked the serenity of being a twosome again. (Even the calm of being alone if that's how it is.) Although your children may not recognize it, you require more tranquility than you used to, and you enjoy it. Yet, at the sound of an SOS, your antenna goes up. You quickly rise to the emergency when your child/adult runs into trouble.

Since you don't know immediately whether your "guest" will be with you just for that stressful night or for a long pull, you had better establish a plan so that your expanded family can make it for the duration. Establish rules of the roost to ensure that everyone has responsibility for its atmosphere. If the living arrangement disintegrates into a maelstrom of annoyances, petty,

*Figure represents women, sixteen years of age or older, who are not housed in institutions. Employment and Earnings, Bureau of Labor Statistics, Census Bureau, September 1984.

**Bureau of Labor Statistics, Employment and Earnings, September 1984.

inconsiderate acts, and little communication between the two of you, your child will leave your home in worse condition than when he reentered, despite your good intentions. He (and you) will feel he has failed again.

Agenda for Action

1. How long?
First discuss "how long?" If you have a comfortable extra room or two, you can be more generous than if your adult child has to bunk on the living room sofa. The disarray will drive you up the wall in short order. Her nerves will fray from lack of privacy and sleep. Start with, "Let's try it for a month or two and then discuss it again."

2. Paying guest or freeloader?
Unless your returning child is broke, discuss a formula for her contribution to the household. Keep up her financial independence by suggesting repayment for food, lodging, laundry, long distance calls, and so on. Be reasonable. A thirty-five-year-old divorcer told us how much he resented that his parents expected him to mow the lawn, shovel the snow, and chauffeur his mother about, in addition to paying rent.

Money can be the number-one trouble spot in a marriage and the tinder box between you and your child. You are probably freer about spending money for your own indulgences than you were while you were paying tuition checks. On the other hand, you know about how far you can stretch your present income without touching principal or savings. If this amount won't cover additional household expenses, how much more will you need?

Will you want to include your child every time you head out for a restaurant, the movies, theater, orchestra? How will you feel about waving good-bye as you depart for a sunny island in frigid February and he is left in the deep freeze alone? Decide ahead of time how to handle these situations rather than offering an emotional, "Come along with us." That doesn't mean that you can't change your mind and break the rules from time to time, just for fun.

3. *We're all in this together.*

Discuss the little, yet momentous, irritations. If you can't stand crushed butts piled high in ashtrays, say so. If you like to go to bed at nine, or after the eleven-o'clock news, talk it over. The stereo and television don't have to be played at ear-splitting decibels. You can close your bedroom door to keep out the still inevitable sound.

4. *This is not a hotel.*

Sure, you want your hurting child and your grandchildren to invite friends to visit. But if the estranged spouse comes to dinner or to stay the night, that might seem asking a lot of you. If you can, stay neutral for this one. If your "hello" sounds more like "get lost," that could spark a battle between the ex-mates, starting with, "From the very beginning, your parents never liked me!" Let them have their reunion without comment from you. It could turn into reconciliation or stepped-up warfare. Wait until after their visit to say your piece. If they plan more get-togethers, you might opt to go to a movie, shut your bedroom door, or turn up the sound on the TV.

When grandchildren are part of the new arrangement, there is great likelihood that the other parent will visit or wait outside for his time with his children. Fair is fair, ex-law or in-law; grandchildren are entitled to, and flourish with, two parents if they can have them.

If a new girlfriend or boyfriend appears fairly regularly, wait a bit before you start a "heart to heart." Your child needs this new relationship, but if this intrudes too much on *your* life in *your* home, say so.

Grandchildren may invite lots of friends to the house. This is a good, healthy sign that they are adjusting to your home. Rules with tolerance are in order. You may love to hear the chatter of young voices, or find the strewn boots, games, toys, and the loud music too wearing.

You have to plan your own social scene more carefully than before, when you could say impulsively to friends, "Come on over for dinner." Your child has to do the same. Work out a comfortable arrangement for "our guests," "your guests," and shared guests.

Household chores are shared. Everybody has to pitch in, because there are increases in cooking, dishes, beds, laundry, cleanup, and lawns. There are many ways to split these up: by chores, by weeks, by payment, or by any combination of these. Don't walk around in silent martyrdom. Get everyone (including grandchildren) involved and helpful.

If you talk over how long, how much, and who does what, you can better adjust and live with overcrowding, overwork, and expense.

Caught Between the Generations

Some middle-aged parents have parents of their own, who draw on them for financial, emotional, and physical support. People in their eighties and nineties are no longer a rarity. When parents of forty, fifty, or sixty have to resume care for their returning adult children and shoulder responsibility for their parents, they are in a viselike bind. How do you achieve a guilt-free moment when your widowed mother is alone, mourning her loss, and your beloved child is grieving over a dead marriage? Unless you settle a big score with yourself and recognize just how far you can extend your psychic and physical well-being to all who draw on it, you will be in a state of perpetual emotional and physical exhaustion.

World War II: A History of Togetherness

In the 1940s, when men went to war and wives went home, Grandma and Granddad often filled in for a missing parent and took their children in. Allotment checks could not cover the expenses of a single family living alone. Perhaps you were the daughter who moved home or the son whose parents made room for your wife and children.

Everyone shared ration stamps and responsibilities. Young wives and sometimes their mothers took jobs in defense plants. It was a patriotic thing to do and the money helped keep the home fires burning. This was the start of women's exodus from the home. At the end of the day everyone hugged the radio, afraid to hear the battle news, unable to ignore it.

One young woman, now in her forties, recalls those years of living with grandparents, missing her dad, and sensing the war-created tensions. When all the adults went off to work she went to a day-care center. She enjoyed the other children and was happy to return to the family hearth each night. She accepted the clearly stated rules of the household, different from those she'd known before. "I remember it as a rather happy time. We stayed until my father came back after VE Day."

Another young woman had more negative memories. She recalls her mother's sadness and tension, having to spend the first two years of her marriage living with in-laws. The daughter recalls other relatives living under the same roof, and being unfavorably compared with one of her baby cousins. The rivalry was so painful that when this young woman grew up and divorced, she would not consider going home to her parents with the children.

Independent Living Together

For those who come home, you hope that this replay of all-under-one-roof will mean a second chance for everyone. It can establish a mature friendship, rich in love and understanding. It can reopen old wounds. There is scarcely a parent who has not wished to take back some days, some nights, some weeks with a child, to redo them. You can't take them back. You must realize that your child is an adult to be revived, not redone. If you think your daughter never really grew up, and you doubt her judgment, you will begin just where you left off, telling her to wear less makeup, criticizing her friends. She will flare with anger and you will feel defensive. If you nag your son with questions he chooses not to answer, prod him about getting his teeth fixed or his suit pressed, the chance for a successful living arrangement, even a short one, is slim. Act like a grown-up, sharing, making your terms clear and negotiating differences.

If after a reasonable time your child refuses to act responsibly, you may have to issue walking papers.

Who Asks Whom?

It is important that your son or daughter initiate the request to live with you, that you don't issue the invitation to them. Many a marital fight whose sights and sounds appear to augur death end in truce. The loving combatants return to each other's arms while you are sorry you ever said, "Come home." You should not set the stage for separation with that invitation. Couples fight, separate, even divorce, and then come together again in their second marriage. Your interference, however well intended, will never be forgotten by the couple. Give your child a warm and loving welcome when he comes home, but don't set it up.

Whose Little Feet?

When grandchildren move in with you, the change in pattern is more extreme than when it is your child alone. They can be anxiety ridden, fearing abandonment after the wild scenes they have witnessed, clinging to mother or father, whoever brought them. These unhappy waifs might pull back from your offerings of rocking, hugs, or food. Wait! You know how quickly they can smile, with tears still wet on their cheeks. In a few days or weeks you might become The Appointed One and only you can diaper them or rock them to sleep. Being the one and only is full of flattery, and exhausting. Children arise before you do, hungry and raring to go. They live in every room and you must move golf trophies, plants, and books to high places. Your living room looks more like a warehouse than your refuge.

You and your returning child have complicated relationships to define. Your child will take care of the grandchildren, but . . . when he or she goes to work or just out, are Grandma and Granddad to be the baby-sitters? You don't have to be. There are preschools, day-care centers, and part- or full-time baby-sitters to be had.

If you do take charge, (1) you have to learn to wear one hat while your child/parent is out and a different one when she is home, at which time he or she becomes "boss" with the children. (Let him or her.) (2) If your son is all thumbs braiding his little girl's hair, does Grandma do it or teach him how? (Teach him.) (3) If your grandson insists that Grandpa put him to bed, guess who gets elected, tired or not? Settle for storytelling, not the long, drawn-out bedtime scene. Bathing small children in a low tub makes for backaches.

With all of them in your home, you will be witness to what kind of parent your child is, day in, day out. That can be the worst torture of all. If you don't like how she does it, we have to tell you what you already know: don't interfere or undermine. There are many ways to raise children and in their young lives there are many influences besides their parents, including grandparents. A good answer for "Who's in charge here?" is: "This is *our* house, those are *your* children."

It is extremely important that you remain grandparents, not parents. It is helpful for grandchildren to have a clear picture of the hierarchy of the family. That means Mom or Dad is central care-giver and authority. Grandma and Grandpa are senators, not cops. It is your right to set rules in your home, but your child has to enforce them with his children. If you don't like what he is doing, discuss it when his offspring are not around. Running to Pop-pop for a "yes, you can go" when Daddy has already said "no" can encourage a child to manipulate and can create warfare in your home.

Relationships break down when generations disagree on rules. A divorcing mother complained that she couldn't stay with her parents much longer because they constantly contradicted her when she reprimanded her son. "Don't be so hard on him," Grandma would say in his presence, or Granddad would scream, "You're making him nervous!" (Translation: "You're making *me* nervous!")

You will have adjustments to make with your grandchildren directly. In the past you probably saw them for visits, days, weekends, vacations. Now it is full-time. They are going to interrupt your routines, wear you down, as much as you love them. They will get to know you, too, as real people with varied emotions and interactions, not fairy godparents showering them with goodies.

Time Out

Some time by yourselves is essential. The first six months of any new job are the most difficult and exhausting. This new/old job can be a killer. If you have to sign off with the grandchildren at 8:00 P.M., say so: "After eight the baby is all yours." Vacations without the brood are a good idea. Your child and grandchild can then have a full-time chance to try it alone. They might like having the house all to themselves.

When you need a brief respite, put a DO NOT DISTURB sign on your door and spend a Saturday in bed surrounded by a month's worth of papers, magazines, and books. Put on a wristband and play tennis. Walk along the river. Don't cook every meal, bring home some take-out dinners.

If you are not the Brunhilde or Ubermensch you once were, and if you suffer fatigue, arthritis, or heart problems, bend your life around these realities. Remind your child that the accelerated pace you are now sustaining adds stress. Talk about it without pushing the guilt button.

Many families work out these intergenerational relationships satisfactorily. Mrs. A. says she and her husband provide shelter and the evening meal. Her unemployed son takes care of his child, dressing him, getting him to school, carting him to friends' homes and birthday parties, in addition to specified household chores. That still gives him time to look for a job.

Roy B., thirty-two, recalls the first postdivorce summer he and his eight-year-old daughter spent with his parents. "It worked out beautifully because Regina went to day camp while I was teaching. Mom and Dad had their life and came and went as always. I had my key to the cottage and responsibility for my daughter. She and I have good memories of Maine. She got to know her grandparents and to love them more. I felt like an adult, not their child, and they didn't find us a burden."

When You Hang Out the No-Vacancy Sign

You may decide that living together, even for a proscribed period, is not for you. There is a touching scene in the play *Dining Room*, by A. R. Gurney, that portrays just such a decision. In this father/daughter confrontation, daughter has come home with three children to announce her divorce. Father is middle-aged, set in his ways. He likes things the way he likes them, wants to have his drink in his pheasant glass in peace and quiet. He can't tolerate the idea of his grandchildren's interference in his life. Daughter is desperate, confused, and wants to come home to find out who she is. She reminisces about her happy childhood, visits to the zoo and the park, to convince him that her place is with him. He is unmoved. He wants her to go back where she belongs, with her husband.

DAUGHTER: "But, Dad, I can't go back."

FATHER: "Neither can I, baby. Neither can I."

7

Money, Money, Money

We never thought we'd have to use the return on our money market funds for one of our daughter's needs. Betty had such a comfortable life before her divorce. She got used to saying "charge it" and can't break the habit. She buys expensive clothes for herself and the kids. She says she needs a car, but she lives right near a shopping center where she can get everything she wants, and someone picks her up and takes her to and from work.

Penny and I are in the happiest time of our married life. The years before our twenty-fifth anniversary were full of stress and in-fighting. We disagreed on how to handle the kids and money. Now the three kids are off on their own, or so we thought, and Penny and I are content. I've begun to take every Friday off and we go to a museum or play golf, have an early dinner out, and just enjoy the evening. But along comes our Betty, angry since her divorce, pleading with us to foot some of her bills, and we just don't want to return to the old pressure cooker. Betty and Bill always lived above their income and we just looked the other way. She couldn't manage on her money then and she can't now. I think Penny and I deserve the luxury of just looking out for ourselves.

—MIKE, BETTY'S FATHER

I can't conceive why my parents make it so hard for me to ask for things I really need and can't afford. They have more money than they could spend in a lifetime. I know they are angry that I had a fling with my boss and blame me for the divorce, but they don't understand how lonely it was, living with a workaholic. Although my affair had a painful ending, I'm glad I did it. They couldn't pay me to go back to waiting for Brian to come home late and tired.

I hate going to my parents for money. They give me such a hard time, it isn't worth it. They think it gives them the right to judge how I spend it, and if I didn't need it so much I'd tell them to stuff it. The difference between my parents and me, my father especially but my mother too, is that they enjoy saving money and I enjoy spending it.

—BETTY

Issues of money and custody dominate the divorce dialogue at home and in court. Right now we are talking Money. In addition to seals, signatures, Latin inscriptions, a "one" in each corner, and a picture of good old George, a dollar bill has at least three strings attached when it passes from parents to children. How easily you give or lend money within your family reflects (1) your perception of your child, (2) your pocketbook, and (3) your values.

Your Perception of Your Child

How you view your child heavily influences your willingness to give or lend him money. If your son always had a cavalier attitude about spending, never saved much, and seemed to have constant debts, you will seriously debate the advisability of lending him a large sum to help him through the rough, expensive divorce period. If your daughter has never made much money and it doesn't seem she ever will, you will think twice before becoming her financier. This is not to say that if you see either son or daughter in dire need you will not help out.

There are children who ask for money and expect it to be handed over unequivocally as proof of love. "You are my parents and it's coming to me! I should be able to fall back on you in need." Some children are too proud to ask for help, and their parents volunteer. Mrs. W. said to us, "How could I enjoy traveling all over the world, knowing that my child had to scrimp to buy clothes for her children?" (That mother gave her daughter a monthly clothing allowance.) Other parents feel their child made his or her own bed and must lie in it. They don't support the divorce, either emotionally or financially.

Mr. Brownstein was an anxious parent. He did not realize that the crucible of marriage and divorce had changed twenty-four-year-old Ruth by sharpening her ability to cope. He and his wife watched their daughter try to be the good guy when her husband's support payments were sporadic and then stopped altogether. Six months after the decree, Mr. Brownstein, a practical businessman, insisted that Ruth instigate court proceedings and sue for nonsupport. He had always thought of her as somewhat weak and in need of prodding to make her stand up for her rights. His big concern was that the major financial responsibility for his grandchildren, ages six and eight, would fall on him.

Ruth resisted his advice. She said she had endured enough anger, courtrooms, and lawyers for a while and wanted to live as normal a life with her children as she could. She would manage somehow; borrow money or try harder to make more as a freelance writer. When Dad kept the pressure on and went so far as to hire a lawyer for her, Ruth displayed a fury alien to his sense of her. She screamed, "Let us alone for a while, and if I do decide to do it, I'll ask for your help!" That was an unexpected response. It gave Dad a new view of his daughter, the realization that divorce had made her grow up in ways marriage never had. They finally talked it out. Mr. Brownstein decided to give his daughter and grandchildren a small monthly supplement for one year. For her part, Ruth agreed to pursue her ex-husband for child support, once she had had a respite from litigation and its headaches.

Another set of parents we interviewed offered to pay the monthly mortgage payments when their daughter Lois divorced and had custody of her child. They knew she could not afford to stay in her home on her salary. They also knew she had to face her economic realities and not become totally dependent on them as she was before she married. Their quick, clear response to Lois's need apparently made everyone feel good. The parents felt they were helping in a substantial, specific way. The daughter appreciated the real boost and decided to sell cosmetics to supplement her income so she could pay the rest of her way.

While you ponder giving or lending you may harbor doubt that your child will pitch in, like Lois, or you may resent that your child spends too freely. If your image of yourself is that of the good guy, galloping in in the white hat, wallet in hand, you might want to think twice. Money can stand for loving, caring, and reinforcement, or it can be a substitute for each, but how it is offered, when, for what, and to which kind of divorcing child must be considered.

Hard Times for Daughters

Your perception of your son's or daughter's economic plight might not take into account some of today's inequities. Despite affirmative action and equal-pay laws, the differences between what men and women earn are a reality.

Women don't get the same return from education and training as men do. A woman with a B.A. or B.S. earns a salary close to that of a man who only finishes eighth grade.

The great majority of working women are lumped into service, clerical, and sales jobs. In Philadelphia, gardeners (male dominated) earn more than practical nurses (female dominated), automotive drivers (male) more than community health workers (female).

The reality of your daughter's financial future is documented by national statistics on her ability to earn, whether she is a professional or on an hourly wage. Men earn more than women for comparable positions.

INCOME FOR MEN/WOMEN

LAWYERS AND JUDGES

Total employed in the United States	524,806
Median income for men	$32,328
Median income for women	$18,503

PHYSICIANS

Total employed in the United States	431,438
Median income for men	$52,918
Median income for women	$22,258

CLERKS—BOOKKEEPING, ACCOUNTING, AND AUDITING

Total employed in the United States	1,827,890
Median income for men	$14,892
Median income for women	$9,883[1]

In a ten-year study, sociologist Lenore J. Weitzman found that aside from income disparity, many women suffer from the no-fault divorce laws adopted since 1970 by most states. On the average, divorced women and the children they care for experience a 73 percent drop in their standard of living the first year after divorce, while the divorced husband's standard of living rises by 42 percent.[2]

The aim of the new divorce laws is to divide marital assets equally between spouses and give the wife enough support to become self-sufficient as soon as possible; this, instead of traditional alimony. Divorce decisions are made at the discretion of each judge. The fact that your son is paying his ex-wife a considerable amount is no guarantee that your divorced daughter will fare well.

It is pie in the sky to expect mothers of young children to become independent in a hurry. Eighty-seven percent of young mothers receive no alimony. The promise of child support is a fiction. They can't collect it. A 1983 report by the U.S. Census Bureau, Department of Commerce, found that only 50 percent of these payments came through. However, when voluntary written agreements were drawn up, 88 percent of the women received regular checks.

Although an increasing number of fathers are pressing for custody, mothers usually assume or are awarded the right to raise the children in their homes. They have to go to work and wrestle with child-care expenses, which can range from $30 to $300 per week. If Mom can find the quintessential Mary Poppins to stay all day and care for the baby at home, the cost can soar.

There is a new catchphrase, "the feminization of poverty." This touches many women, college educated and upper middle class, down through the economic spectrum to chronically poor. It has been said that poverty is only a divorce away for large numbers of women.

> I can't believe the reality. I thought that after Mike and I split apart the kids and I would live pretty much the way we always had. The harsh truth is that we watch every penny, eat cheaper, and have much less of everything.

Don't be misled by the hope of alimony. Two factors supersede the wife's income and occupation: the husband's income and the duration of the marriage. Spouses of men who earn $30,000 per year or more are more likely to be awarded alimony (62 percent) than those whose husbands make less than $20,000 (15 percent).[3]

Recognizing men and women as equal at divorce times does not take into account their separate treatment in the world where they live and work. Your daughter almost surely started her career disadvantaged in earning power. She may have had to sacrifice advancement opportunities because her husband's career came first. When women work they almost always have two full-time jobs, an income only from the one outside the house.

Your Son's Finances

We recognize that the money-management picture for daughter-divorcer is difficult, unfair, and often very bleak. What about son-divorcer? Statistics show that he can earn more for comparable work than a woman in the same profession or job. If the U.S. figures for median support relate to the order handed down to your son, it seems he should have plenty of disposable income for renting another house, purchasing his same brand of cognac, and flying off to the Caribbean when winter is blustery. This does not always compute.

One grandfather who earns $90,000 annually as a neurosurgeon related how he helped his son and daughter-in-law while they were married and must continue now that they are divorced:

> Jonathan and Elise were married during his second year of residency. His future seemed assured. Very attractive, she worked as a model-salesperson in a fashion shop, made very little money, no pension or other benefits, but she loved it. They lived high, and we enjoyed the notion that they were the perfect couple. When their two children reached preschool age, the cost of running the household without private-school tuition was $60,000. Since we were able to give each member of the family $6,000 a year as a nontaxable gift, we did it. We could easily afford it and we enjoyed providing the extra leeway it gave them.
>
> Now the marriage is over—for whatever reason. Maybe it's better. We realized they fought as much as they loved. My son has to give his ex-wife $60,000 a year to run the household in the way it had been run. Nothing has changed because he is not

in residence. How can he live on the remaining money he makes, pay rent or perhaps buy a house, have a few luxuries, unless we help out even more than we did when he was married?

—JACOB S., age 66
Minneapolis

One couple told the story of their son whose marriage was rife with his wife's wild temper tantrums, often punctuated with a bottle heaved through a window. On one occasion, she slashed her fur coat. She tried therapy but abandoned it time after time until finally their son had to take temporary refuge with his parents. The children of this marriage seemed comfortable staying behind with their mother. Although she has a master's degree in library science, she has never been able to hold a job and it is unlikely that she ever will.

The judge granted the wife $20,000 a year in alimony and $10,000 a year in child support, indicating that the alimony might have to be continued for her lifetime since she had no other resources.

These parents went on to explain that their son works as a research chemist and the money he paid toward the support of his children and ex-wife left him with $15,000 a year. They converted their comfortable two-story home into a duplex and gave him the second floor rent-free. His parents respected his privacy and he respected theirs. Without their understanding help, this son would have faced a marginal existence.

Fathers' and Children's Equality, a Philadelphia-based fathers' rights group, sets out a plan for action in its 1986 newsletter. Among other things, they ask for new laws requiring that wives who are awarded substantial court-ordered child support payments be held accountable for how the money is spent.

The same newsletter rails against inequitable distribution of property following divorce.

Only now it will not be merely wages that are collected, but rather your pension, your business profits or earnings resulting from academic degrees in law, medicine, or whatever. With little regard for whose ingenuity, brains, or hard work attained these assets, the laws and the courts now are defining them as marital property to be owned and divided between the parties to the marriage just like any other property. The trend is part of the mounting pressure to ensure that men will continue to be life-time meal tickets who will keep divorced wives with no work effort on their part and regardless of rights and wrongs, in the style to which they became accustomed during marriage.[4]

The matter of alimony is murky for men as well as for women. It does seem clear that if your son is upper middle class, he has a better than average chance of having to pay for his wife's sustenance after divorce. So, no matter what, son or daughter, there are inequities all around in this chaotic world of divorce. You must take them all into account as you tote up what help you may or may not offer.

Your Pocketbook: What Do They Think We're Made of, Money?

We take it for granted, and so does your child, that your impetus to give comes from being a loving parent. The dilemma is, your love may be limitless but your pocketbook isn't. Love and money are an awkward mix, and you need to temper your feeling with some realistic considerations.

When you determine that money is absolutely needed, ask your son or daughter to calculate the time ahead when he or she can repay. Obtain a promissory note for any money you lend. Let him or her explore other areas where emergency money could be obtained. The goal is to help your child/adult over a financial rough spot, not put yourself in charge of his or her life and foster dependency. Lending or giving money grants you no right to control the divorcer's actions, either financial or social. When a bank lends money there is no surveillance on anything except repayment. A banker never asks "Why, when you owe so much money, are you wearing a new designer coat?" but you might.

You do have some rational choices to make when you feel you must open your pocketbook to help your divorcer. There is short-term help, an outright gift, or a loan, whatever you feel you can afford. Be advised, the number who actually repay family loans is small. The guilt of the borrower and the resentment of the lender are large and can create a chasm between you and your child.

The Wellers lived to regret a generous gesture they made many years before:

> We were once considered affluent. We had a big house, two cars, and were able to put our kids through college, our son through architecture school. When Bill got married, we gave them $30,000 toward the construction of their house. It gave us great pleasure to help out that way. That was sixteen years ago and things were rosy.
>
> Bill and Trudy are in the throes of a divorce now. Their kids are twelve and fourteen. When their marriage began to fail my husband had just retired. Next he had a severe stroke. I am very crippled with arthritis and can't take care of him. We have round-the-clock nurses. We are selling our stocks and bonds like crazy to pay for his care. We are near the end of our resources.
>
> Trudy wants to stay in the house with the children. We want Bill to insist that they sell it so they can return the money we gave as a down payment so willingly long ago. We need it to pay our bills. I know our son is paying alimony and child support. He could use that money from the house and so could we. Trudy has her salary and the money from Bill and she'd get a fair amount of her share from the sale of the house, too.
>
> I keep asking him if he's talked to his lawyer about this. He continues to put me off. I know Trudy is giving him a very

difficult time and he doesn't want to introduce our problems on top of his. The trouble is we never thought about getting a note from them. Trudy blames us for the divorce and has no intention of repaying us. We're going to have to hire our own lawyer and really can't afford it.

Those parents were trusting and naïve not to have a written record of the $30,000. The best that mother can hope for is that her son will address his parents' problem when the heat of his divorce simmers down. By then it may be too late in terms of some of the present, urgent decisions that need to be made. When your child's divorce occurs, you may find yourself with some of the unkindest cuts of all.

For the short term it is better to help out with money for a specific need. Some parents like to wipe out the charge-card debts and provide their child with a fresh start. Others decide on a year's rent or school tuition for their grandchildren. Whether it is a gift or a loan, money that is earmarked for a specific purpose reduces the possibility of misunderstandings between you and your child. You won't feel used by your child's spending your money in ways you judge extravagant. You won't feel tempted to inflict your values with a strings-attached edge.

If you are thinking of promising to continue to help, remember that both your financial circumstances and your child's can change in the future. Your son or daughter may get a better job or remarry within a year. There is more of a chance that a person younger than you can look forward to an increased income as time goes by.

It is better to think Temporary. If you encourage dependence on your money, your child could become insatiable, since it is easy money and he or she may feel it does not have to be accounted for. In most instances, long-term help could cost you tax dollars. Unless your expenditure represents more than 50 percent of your child's support, you cannot claim him or her as a dependent.

Whatever you do, don't mortgage your own future. This may

mean explaining to your divorcer that you just finished paying for his or her graduate school and you don't want to be on the hook again because of the decision to divorce. You are entitled to maintain the quality of your life, and today's statistics are stretching the limits of longevity further and further. Plan accordingly.

How you give or withhold money deeply affects your relationship with your child. If you are loaded with guilt over your son's behavior and think all his failures are your fault, you may overreact. If you are angry about your daughter's divorce, believe her to be responsible for the debacle, you may be stingy.

Make the act of giving money pleasurable for you as well as for your child and the grandchildren:

• Take your grandchildren on a clothes-shopping junket. That feels good!
• Plan a weekend in the country or at the shore with your child and grandchildren.
• Take your grandchildren to dinner and a movie once a week. (You choose the film one week, they, the next.)

As you walk the landmines around the divorce, remember that almost any well-intentioned act can boomerang. If you attach strings to money or gifts, your child or ex-law will be angry and your joy in giving will be lost. If you mimic some friends' gesture, try to do what they have done for their divorcer, and it is alien to your values, look out! Giving a lavish gift, such as vacation money or a fur coat, to keep up with your particular Joneses may leave you with resentment and regret. If you take your grandchildren to the shore for a month thinking it will be your vacation, too, you may be disappointed and emotionally and financially spent.

Being sensitive about the way you give is a two-way street. Many children do expect to depend on parents after they leave home. This newly divorced daughter and this overstrapped son clearly perceive their parents' dilemma.

They worry because my life is so unsettled and because I don't make enough money. They would like me to marry again soon, someone who would make them feel I wasn't alone, and they would not have to be there to back me up in case I suddenly become destitute. They feel it is an added responsibility. It is really the financial thing they worry about. They think they have to help me in ways they didn't before divorce. I'm sorry about it, but I do need them to be there right now.

—LAUREL

If I had known how expensive it is to divorce, I'd have thought twice about getting married. Claire doesn't earn a cent. She's fighting my selling the house, so I can't even get my hands on half that money. I have to pay support for the kids, and those legal costs are killing. I hate to pay the current high rates for a loan, but how can I ask my parents to lend me money? They are just beginning to enjoy leisure after years of hard work. I can't put pressure on them now. I'll just have to go to see my friendly banker and bite the bullet.

—STEVE

Time Is Money

If you can't or won't give or lend money, there are creative ways to help that cost almost nothing. If your child has custody, there are trips to the dentist, to guitar lessons, to school events, or staying home with a feverish child that take time out from his or her work day and can even jeopardize a job. This is true for fathers and mothers alike. The film 1979 *Kramer vs. Kramer* dealt realistically with the problems of a custodial father and showed how child care without a mate has its frazzling aspects. Grandparents can help in many ways.

You can give first aid by doing some of the chauffeuring of your grandchildren. You can spend evenings with them, at your house or theirs, so that your daughter can go out to dinner. Even if your son does not have custody of the children, he can use some of this same kind of assistance when they come to him for their regular visits. Sometimes baby-sitting, chauffeuring, or just having a good time with your grandchildren can be more of a boon than money.

Other ways to pitch in with your divorcer:

1. Prepare meals for warmups in your divorcer's oven, if he or she is a working parent or a sick one.

2. If he or she is sick, by all means take the kids off his or her hands for a while and give your child a chance to recover.

3. If neither parent can take time off, you can be in the audience for your grandchild's school play. One grandparent flew eight hundred miles for this. "It was the most expensive theater ticket I ever bought!" she said. "And the most enjoyable."

4. If your child is expecting an important call, offer to wait for it at his house, or tell him to give your phone number as an alternative.

5. Same as above for parcel deliveries. Offer to wait at his house or yours.

6. Your child probably has a variety of phone calls to make in a day: inquiries about jobs, camps, doctor and dentist appointments, baby-sitting arrangements, the cost of a computer, a phone-bill error. Offer to make some of them.

7. If you are handy at home repairs, that saves money and the discomfort of waiting for the repairman. As a bonus, let a grandchild watch. Let her handle your tools; teach him how to fix. If you are not handy, offer to wait for the plumber, exterminator, et al. You have to be a saint to offer that one!

8. If you knit or sew, you can save your divorcer lots of money and make your grandchildren look special. You can just mend and darn if you can't make garments. Let your grandchild watch these operations, too.

9. Help read insurance forms, tax forms, and other small-print legal agreements, assuming that your eyes are still good enough.

10. Are there pets? You may be needed to walk the dog or take an alligator to the vet. Pet-sitting may be second only to baby-sitting in importance.

Just as we endorse giving money without strings attached, we recommend baby-sitting without any requirements for how your child (or ex-law) uses that respite time. One daughter reported great resentment toward her parents because they agreed to baby-sit only when she had a date with a man. Other evenings, when she wanted to join her women friends to go bowling or out for a drink, her parents told her she ought to stay home, the kids needed her. That did not prevent this daughter from paying others to sit on those precious few evenings, but it created hard feelings, which even the children picked up on.

Your Values: What Is Important to You

My parents' generation are the kind of people who escaped into a private, idealized suburban existence—a home of their own, a garden, several TV sets, and a freezer full of the basic needs for survival. We were the props for this fantasy . . . the perfect family. Their generation rarely divorced. We were brought up to believe in their dream and duplicate it, but we can't.

LILA, 39 years old

We who raised families in the forties, fifties, and sixties probably did set an upscale standard for our children. A study commissioned by the Congressional Joint Economic Committee reveals that the baby boom generation, now in their thirties, find they cannot match their parents' middle-class achievements of nice homes, financial security, and children's education. ". . . In some ways, 1973 was the last good year," say the authors Frank S. Levy, Professor of Public Affairs at the University of Maryland, and Richard Michel, Director of Income Security and Pension Policy Center at the Urban Institute in Washington (1984).

It is often hard for parents to understand how the kind of atmosphere we created in our homes affected our children, how the messages we hoped to transmit were retranslated by our young into standards different from what we intended them to be. Divorce was not on our agenda, nor was the sharp reduction in income that often follows.

It is probably during your child's marital separation that many of you learn for the first time just how the couple lived, how their income was spent. Until now it was none of your business; you didn't ask and you weren't told. But now there are adjustments to make—some trimming-downs and some living-withouts—and you discover that your and your child's values lie poles apart. You believe in security; he or she wants fulfillment. He or she doesn't want to scrimp and save for an earned tomorrow; you think that is important. It is likely you think your divorcing couple spent too much money when together, and it seems each wants to maintain the same spending habits now that they are living separately.

An Illinois father laments:

Bud is asking for a loan again. He hasn't paid me back yet for the last one. My son says his bills are doubled since his separation. I think Lucy has him over a barrel. She says she needs a new TV; the old one is not worth fixing. I think she just wants remote control and stereo sound. She claims the set is for Luke, their little boy. I haven't heard him complain. In addition to her new demands, Bud has piles of unpaid bills from the time they all lived together, the mortgage on the lake house, payments on the two cars, et cetera, et cetera, et cetera. She wants him to pay them all off before the divorce settlement. There is no way he can.

I know all about my son's extra needs now, including his separate apartment with a bedroom for his son when he comes on the weekends. I lent Bud a few thousand dollars right after they split up. Suddenly I've decided I can't continue to keep my son, his estranged wife, and my grandson afloat. We gave Bud an education. He has a job. She works. Why should I have to foot their bills?

That father loaned his son money to spend as he saw fit, with no strings attached. That is something we recommend, but the story illustrates how the point at which your divorcer asks for money is often a moment of truth. It highlights the difference in values between you and yours. It forces you to face your feelings and decide what is important to you. Just as your child's adolescence was a time of testing, when you were forced to take a stand about new behaviors, so divorce puts you on the spot and pushes you toward self-definition.

You may have always viewed yourself as a generous parent and now feel selfish at drawing the line. You may have thought you trusted your child 100 percent and then find you care where and to whom the money you give goes. You may find yourself asking, "If I give it to my son now, will he be there for me when I need him?" A question you never wanted to ask.

One moment of truth is when your grandchildren are coming for an overnight and ask you to buy the pajamas. Suddenly you feel caught in the crossfire of the divorcers' monetary battle and find yourself pondering how much your grandchildren are your financial responsibility. One grandfather told his grandson who had been coached by his mother to ask him for new clothes, "Grandma and I are for the good things. Your mom and dad give you necessities: food, clothes, a place to live. We are here for the goodies." In making his decisions, that grandfather considered his son's good income, the adequate child support his ex-law was getting, and his own self-interest. Instead of clothes, he sent plane fare for a visit to Pop-pop and Grandma, making it clear to one and all how he feels about supporting his grandchildren.

Compare that to another grandparent who felt infuriated and full of spite: "I won't give that bitch one dime to send my grandson to overnight camp. I don't care if he has to stay home. You know why? I don't want to make his mother's life one bit easier." That grandparent acted out of revenge, not something we recommend. To deny contributing to the development and pleasure of an eleven-year-old is something you cannot redo later on. In addition, if your refusal leads to more hostility, the chance for a workable relationship between you and your ex-law becomes more remote than ever.

There is another part to this puzzle of grandchildren and money: how the other set of grandparents behaves. If they give your grandchildren more grandiose material things than you feel are appropriate or can afford, don't get into the competition. Hold on to your values and your pocketbook. You will be sending an important message to your grandchildren on the relative importance of "things," especially if you share yourself, your time, your love with them.

A grown granddaughter looks back:

> I had an exceptional relationship with my one grandmother and it had nothing to do with money. She never demanded anything of me, yet I always wanted to be near her, to help her. I can remember spending a whole day shelling peas for canning at her side and feeling so happy, and that's what matters.

Money for Ex-Laws

It might be that the best way you can materially help your grandchildren is to help your divorcer maintain a decent standard of living. This could even be extended to your ex-law if he or she has custody.

You generally can't provide long-term support to ex-laws, but special conditions may create exceptions. Occasionally we interviewed parents who were fed up with their irresponsible divorced child. In one case, a son paid inadequate child support and ignored his children. After asking their son for permission to help the ex-wife and grandchildren and being refused, his parents finally offered the ex-law both money and an invitation for every holiday.

A widowed New York grandmother felt the need to keep the ties with her ex-law:

> When my son and his wife separated, my major concern was for their children. The divorcers were tough and took care of themselves. It would have been easier to forget about my ex-daughter-in-law. She never was comfortable in our family, but I had my values straight. I wanted closeness to my grandson and granddaughter and my son understood. Since the kids lived with my ex, I could not ignore her. I courted her, included her in family parties, asked for her every time I phoned my grandchildren. I even sent her money gifts from time to time for extras and, frankly, to cement our relationship. It's working for me and we are doing just fine.

Your ex-son-in-law could be ill, unable to work, and you might be moved to help. Talk to your daughter and hope she can understand your need to give him a boost. Emergencies present special circumstances, and if he has no one else to call upon, you might want to volunteer this one last time. Your daughter may even be relieved from the guilt of having left him while he's down.

In New Mexico, the parents of a daughter who had walked out on her husband and child, and disappeared, sent money to their ex-son-in-law to support the children. His job at the post office was sufficient when his wife contributed her salary to the family budget, but now he finds it hard to get the kids the things they need as they grow up—clothes, books, braces for the little girl's teeth. That check from the grandparents makes a real difference.

Great-grandmother's Ring

Besides the unreturned loans you can kiss good-bye, there is also great-grandmother's ring and other family heirlooms. Many ex-daughters-in-law keep jewelry and furniture that were in your family for generations. Deciding who got the car was a source of disappointment to this elderly father: "Last year I bought the children a car. The money I had was limited and couldn't be replaced, but at my age it gave me pleasure to think I could still give them something they needed. Then they decided to divorce. If I had known my son wouldn't get the car, I certainly wouldn't have bought it. I feel very sorry now."

It's up to you to talk to your divorcer and make your concerns known. He or she probably won't want to hear them, claiming they will only prolong the process and make it more difficult, but like it or not you are the silent partner(s) to this divorce. Your emotional and financial interests must be voiced to and through your child at the time of separation. Be tactful but firm and get your licks in early.

Where There's a Will

In most instances, there is little you can do to salvage past gifts and loans, but there's a great deal you can and must do to protect your future interests. Divorce is a time to dig into your safety deposit box and reread the "of sound minds" and "give and bequeaths." You need to be sure that whatever you leave to posterity will stay in your family. As you read the following list of possible questions for your lawyer, remember not to decide to scrimp now or to mortgage your future to ensure that there will be an inheritance for the children later. (A good lawyer won't let you.) You have to assess your own needs, take care of yourselves.

1. How can I be sure my child's ex- does not get any part of the money I leave my son or daughter?

2. How can I best express my wishes to be sure my ex-law does not get control of the money I leave my grandchildren?

3. How can I have my will written to be sure that grandchildren born after my divorcer's remarriage are protected?

4. If any of my grandchildren should die, how can I assure that their mother or father (my ex-law) cannot get to the money I left for them?

5. How can I best extricate myself from business or professional involvement with my ex-law?

The answers to these questions are crucial. You are in a new position now and the family money and assets must be protected. If you ever believed that divorce pertained only to the nuclear couple, money is the most tangible proof that this is not so. Make no mistake about it. At this time, your child is not the only one who needs a good lawyer.

Communication—Talking It Over

Money is a touchy topic, yet it behooves you now to talk about it with your separated child. It is important to find out how much in debt he or she may be, how realistic he or she is about his or her life-style-to-come, and to tell your child just where you are financially. Your discussion should involve how you succeeded in keeping the family solvent, your present income, and your own plans for this part of your life. Then, when you decide whether and what to give, your child can understand your motivations. Don't place yourself in the position of martyr. Just state as honestly as you can where you are financially and find out exactly where he or she is. You are on sensitive territory and the conversation may be awkward.

Consider the timing of your discussion. You may be tempted to broach the subject before you are even asked, the same sort of overeagerness you may show by offering more than you can afford. Bide your time and watch for the signs that your child is ready to talk. The signal could be a complaint or worry about money or a mention of needing to look for a job.

Some adult children still take their parents for granted, looking upon them as the once and future provider, never having questioned where their money came from. Perhaps you paid college tuition and funded the big-scale wedding on borrowed money and it is high time your child is made aware of it. A tactful way of saying this is, "I never told you before, but I think it's appropriate to discuss it now."

Talking it over is almost always just a beginning. The topic of money will arise between you again and again, sometimes at your instigation, sometimes at his or hers. In time it will be less upsetting, and the more you discuss it the clearer the understanding between you will become. A new respect for each other's point of view will probably emerge.

The Other Children

While you are at it, consider your other children. They need some talks, too. If you appear to be overcompensating your distressed child, your other children might feel angry and alienated. Although they might not be among the presently grieving, their expectation of considerations, gifts, and help from you is probably just beneath the surface. Handing over your second car to single-again daughter turns off Jimmy, her elder brother. ("My wife has to depend on neighbors for all the car-pooling. I'm a salesman and must have the car every day. Why isn't our need as great as my sister's just because she's separated?") Taking on the burden of son Jeff's second-household rent distresses his sisters. ("Our parents are scooping into their own money. Who will pick up the slack if they need costly medical care?")

Financial decisions usually affect the whole family, not just you and the divorcer. Family members need one another in time of crisis; yet, money can be divisive, arousing jealousy and ancient sibling rivalry. Talk to your other children one by one. Explain your decisions to them and give them the same kind of information about the family finances as you gave your child-in-need. Hear them out. Assure them that if they have a crisis or a special need you will surely be there for them.

Sharing the attitudes of your children can provide some new understanding. Your children will learn things about you and your financial position that they might never have known. You may learn things about them you never knew. Caution! Free and full sharing of information can cause new questions to arise in each family member's mind that are not easily answered. It can uncover hidden animosities, open up old wounds, provoke fresh causes for anger. At first glance, this may appear negative, but it is better to try to soften hard feelings through discussion than to pretend they don't exist. Ignoring them only causes them to reappear during other crises.

It may be that an open discussion will be a tremendous relief for your family. Your children may feel reassured about your future and theirs. Sometimes, when they understand the financial binds, brothers and sisters offer help from their own bank accounts.

At divorce time, money can be a boon or a bust, a bone of contention or a pipe of peace. Your decisions are not made in a vacuum; your other children's eyes are watching, even if they are thousands of miles away. The main issues for you are: what your divorcer needs, what you have, whether he or she warrants your help, and what you want to give. One thing is sure, you will all agree that money matters.

1. Bureau of Census, U.S. Dept. of Commerce 1980.

2. Weitzman, Lenore J., *The Divorce Revisited* (The Free Press, division of Macmillan, 1985).

3. Child Support and Alimony, 1983, U.S. Dept. of Commerce, Bureau of Census.

4. Newsletter, Fathers' and Children's Equality, 1986.

8

There's No Such Thing As an Ex-Grandparent

Your Grandchildren—the Shuttle Generation

The first time I saw those children in the airport, they puzzled me. Sometimes just one alone, sometimes two together, but not messing around, not wild, just waiting. It was about two years ago, on a plane from Chicago to Los Angeles, that I recognized just who they were. Two children, a boy about six and a girl perhaps two years older, were placed in the seats across the aisle by the stewardess. I noticed them particularly because the little boy sat with his coat buttoned way up to his neck for the whole journey. No parent, no grandparent or friend came to make him more comfortable for the trip. I'm a mother hen at heart and wanted to ease the coat from his back, kind of settle the discomfort I sensed in him, but these days you hesitate about helping.

In the Los Angeles airport, the stewardess escorted the children to an anxious young man who stooped to enfold both in his arms. Neither child returned the fervor of his embrace. Suddenly, the whole ugly truth hit me. These children split their time between mother and father, and were still numb with the aftermath of separation. ("If I hug Daddy too much, will Mom be upset? Why can't we all live in one house the way we used to?")

This year I'm the one who sees my grandchildren shuttled between my son and their mother. They separated just six weeks ago, and my outgoing little grandchildren have become silent, unresponsive, and, so far, they are not playing like two little kids should. They are the byproducts of a society in turmoil. Thousands of the children of divorce ride the jet streams, moving from mother to father, reaching in bureau drawers for the pj's in this house, listening for sounds of children who live nearby that house. I know how I feel when I've vacationed too long and yearn for my own bed, my own pot of coffee. How are these kids adjusting to one bed here, one bed there, and their parents separated forever?

MARILYN S., CHICAGO

Where do you grandparents fit along the routes your grandchildren travel? When do you get a chance to be somebody to those shuttled children in the way you were only yesterday, as you expected to be throughout your lifetime?

You are the foundation of the family and represent what being older means, especially to the little ones. Their attitudes toward aging are patterned on how they perceive you. You give them a particular kind of attention and are more indulgent than their parents are and they love it! To you, being a grandparent is one of the bonuses of passing into middle age and having grown-up, married children. You keep pictures available to let everyone know just how special these grandchildren are to you.

While you are struggling to regain your footing on unfamiliar family ground, and facing a once-loving couple now locked in combat, you have many questions, not the least of which is, "Now what happens to our grandchildren?"

Your impassioned pleas to "give it one more chance, forgive and forget, stay together for the children's sake" have fallen into a cacophonous echo chamber along with, "Why don't you try a family counselor?" Their marriage is among the discards of a throw-away society and you have no control over the situation.

You refuse to be cast out too. You intuitively know what a study of freshman students at Wichita State University and the University of Texas revealed regarding their attitudes toward grandparents: Only 4 percent felt neutral; the remaining 96 percent considered their grandparents "extremely important" or "important" in their lives. Ninety percent wished they had seen their grandparents more than they did.[1]

> Grandmother was just accepting. She had a certain level of empathy no other relative of mine had. She thought like a child and knew what a child appreciates. She would lay out special little treats for me, even if they were carrot sticks cut a certain way but they were the way I wanted them cut, and she would do it. She's still here, and I love having my daughter visit her great-grandmother.
>
> ELLEN B.

You are keenly aware that as you reach out to your grandchildren they are getting something unique that they don't receive from any other people in their lives.

Grandparents and parents respond differently in their judgment of a child's actions. Parents view each growing stage with its negatives and positives as the one that will be frozen forever. Grandparents recognize the waves of change from impish and naughty to loving and compliant as stages along the way to adulthood.

When Johnny steals coins from the kitchen honey jar, parents worry that he will end up a delinquent. They are too close to the situation. Grandparents, from the perspective of time and experience, are aware that most children take money sometimes to secrete in pockets for the jingling sound or for some forbidden treat. "All kids snitch something when they are growing up." Grandparents make every day a holiday when grandchildren visit. Parents consider it a day off when they sneak off alone and someone else takes the kids. Parents can't wait for the next stage. They want crawling to move up to walking, infant sounds to separate into words, and the grungy little boy to turn into a well-groomed youngster. Grandparents know that each stage is all too brief and they are happy to once more hold a small hand, cut up the hamburger, and respond to each "Why?"

They Need Your Stability

Your grandchildren feel love and acceptance from you just because they were born into your family. Dr. Arthur Kornhaber, president of the Foundation for Grandparenting, in Jay, New York, who calls grandparents "the big lap, the safety net," defines the bond between grandparents and grandchildren second only in emotional power to the bond between parent and child.[2] The stable link that holds the bond is often a lifeline because they feel so bereft when their parents divorce. These are the times when you are the best source for the succor and support they need. During the first days you must move cautiously, with sensitivity and tact. It is a good idea just to be supportive for a while before opening up any dialogue, to watch that discussions are always on their cue, not yours. Wait for an opportune moment to test the waters. If your grandchild seems receptive and has been storming about how terrible he or she feels, you can reveal that you share the grief that Mom and Dad are no longer together.

1. Respond, don't initiate such a conversation.

2. Ask their parents (preferably both, or your own child if you can't communicate with your ex-law) how they have explained the separation and be guided by that. Your question might initiate a parent-child discussion if the self-absorbed divorcers have not thought about how your grandchild feels.

3. Gear your comments to the child's age. Don't get into too complicated an interchange. Make it clear that no one is to blame, that the roots of the divorce lie in the relationship of two people, the parents. Reassure your uneasy grandchild that nothing he or she did could have caused the rift. Though the words you speak may not directly assuage your grandchild's

unhappiness, the fact that the subject is not verboten, that it can be talked about between you, is a relief. The mutual respect that makes such a discussion possible has to be a plus.

Grandparents are often teachers and mentors for their grandchildren. You show them your code of morality by action and word. If you are asked, you can give advice on some perplexing questions they have at this unhappy hour.

You can help them look beyond themselves, play with them, teach them the wonders of life. You have a sense of proportion about what they do since you raised one of their parents and his or her brothers and sisters. You don't panic as quickly as their parents do when the child falls from grace. You've seen it all before.

Grandparents are the link with the past that gives children the sense that the family was here before and will continue to thrive. If you tell stories of your childhood and of the growing-up years of their father or mother, they will beg to hear them again if you keep them brief and lively.

One young man of twenty-six, who had just attended his grandfather's funeral, reminisced: "No matter what I did and what I wore, my grandfather loved me. He was a shining beacon in my life. During one Easter vacation, I helped him plant spring flowers and fix the hose. It was better than playing baseball!"

Are your grandchildren the fall guys? All too clearly you see their suffering. They have lost confidence in their parents ("Are these angry people the ones who are supposed to take care of me?"); and the first months following the separation are the worst for the couple, their children, and you. You, Grandma and Grandpa, could hold the key to the only stability in their upside-down world. Visiting you is a return to well-known turf where the scents, the bathroom towels, and the toys are all familiar. Your home is not the battleground. You have not changed.

In 1980 Judith S. Wallerstein and Jean Berlin Kelly studied 131 children of divorced families in the Chicago area who agreed to participate in a six-week counseling program. The overwhelming effect of divorce on these children was shock, fear, and grief. Less than 10 percent were relieved by their parents' decision to separate despite the screaming fights they might have heard. When grandparents lived nearby, the children were considerably consoled by their presence, but three-quarters of those studied had no grandparents close enough geographically to provide the "big lap."[3]

Children under five years of age coped successfully with their parents' divorce in many ways, but those in the six-to-eight-year group showed pervasive sadness. Boys especially grieved for their absent father and singled out their custodial mother with accusations that she had caused the divorce. The nine-to-twelve-year groups tried to understand it all. They displayed an air of bravado and disbelief. These "middle-aged" youngsters reached out to others and kept compulsively busy to avoid thinking about the tremendous changes in their families.

Distress among adolescents paralleled that of their parents. Teenagers constantly vacillate between taking steps toward maturity and retreating to childish behavior. Being on the brink of trying their wings but with one foot firmly in the door, these older children find no one at home to help them. One parent has left, the other is busy trying to cope, and both are totally consumed by their own problems. In the Wallerstein study, adolescents revealed that they now perceived Mom and Dad as separate individuals, not the omnipotent, idealized twosome of an earlier time. The teenagers appeared to have been catapulted into premature independence, their growing up considerably accelerated.

Dr. Wallerstein's investigation, the longest study to date of divorced families, lists nine worry questions common to most children. We have suggested some responses for concerned grandparents:

1. *"Who will take care of me?"* You can, at intervals or for a period of time. Adolescents need a kind of baby-sitting, too.

2. *"Is there anything in the world reliable and predictable?"*

Grandparents should make special efforts to be there for them as promised, every time, barring emergencies. When you say you're going to pick them up or meet them, get there and on time. Your reliability is crucial.

3. *"Are my parents crazy?"* When the opportune moment arises, you can explain what an unsettling period this is for both parents and that after a while they and you will settle down more and more.

4. *"Where is my father/mother now living?"* Encourage visits to the absent parent's home if that meets with the plans of the divorcers. The child wants to touch the new base in order to feel part of the new setting.

5. *"Will my mother/father—my only parent—get sick, hit by a car, or worse?"* You can't promise this won't happen, but let your grandchild know that you are a backup and so are the cousins, uncles, and aunts from both sides of the family.

6. *"Will we have enough money now?"* Reassure the child that he or she will be taken care of. You can help with money or gifts to your grandchild, giving a weekly allowance or money for a class trip.

7. *"Will I have to change schools now?"* Tell them that many children remain where they are and attend the same school, but if change is in the wind, research the positives in the new school and visit the classroom if you can.

8. *"Will I have to move to a new neighborhood?"* Recount the stories of the times you moved, your new room, new friends, and the yard for a dog. Offer reassurance that the old friends can visit and stay overnight.

9. *"Is Mom going to marry Bob? Will they keep me with them?"* You probably can't do much about this one except wonder with them.

Your grandchildren may never directly voice these particular doubts, but instead may act out their worries by beating up a best friend or withdrawing into isolation from friends and family.

When your grandchildren grieve for their lost home life, or strike out in anger, there is no magic word or situation you can produce to dispel their feelings. Margaret Adams Greenlee, a social worker at Sloan-Kettering Cancer Center in New York City, reports "that children mourn intermittently and longer than adults. They can't sustain a long period of emotional stress, so they do it in short spurts." Although this study relates directly to children's response to death in the family, we believe it applies to their heartache when parents divorce. Their grief pattern may be totally different from yours. Just when you think your mourning is abating, they may pick up again on theirs.

The Ones Who Avoid You

In spite of all the stability you represent, some children may surprise you by not making a beeline to your home, your arms. They may find all relationships suspect, (if one failed, will all of them disintegrate?) or may withdraw and refuse to accept your solace.

They have many reasons for maintaining a distance from you.

One is their need for secrecy. Not even grandparents can be told about all the strife, the yelling, the threats they have witnessed. If the grandchildren don't say it with words, the nightmare might not be true. Once the words are out, the breakup becomes a threatening reality.

Two is any guilt your grandchild might feel about having caused the separation. Just as you might be torturing yourself about whether your criticism of the couple's high-priced foreign car could have sparked the final argument, your little one might have gnawing fears that his disobedience, or his four-letter words that infuriated his parents, might have driven them apart. Like you, your grandchild harbors this guilt deep inside.

One grandfather, a few years after the divorce, finally understood the intensity of his grandson's displaced guilt:

Seven-year-old Phillip was a bed wetter. His dad was extremely annoyed when he crept through the darkness seeking comfort and a dry bed. He knew he disturbed his parents as he cuddled beside them. His mother rubbed his back and held him. His dad grumbled, "He's too old for this kind of thing. You spoil him! I'll be tired for work tomorrow and so will you." His mother would then walk Phil back to his room, urging a stop at the bathroom before he settled back on the dry side of the bed. Sometimes she had to change all the sheets. Phil's big sister always wrinkled her nose when she came into his room. He had to find excuses when his friend Bud asked why he didn't want to go to overnight camp with him. Phil hated himself for the nightly puddle over which he felt he had no control.

When Phil's parents argued loudly in the night, he listened to hear if he was blamed for all the loss of sleep and extra work he caused. At breakfast time either the washer or dryer spinning his wet sheets was constantly making noise so that everyone had to shout to be heard.

One day he came home from school and the house looked strange! The wedding picture of his mother and father was gone from the living room table. One closet in his parents' bedroom was stripped bare, and the wooden valet where his dad's jacket usually hung was gone. Last night's fight had been the one to end all fights and his father had moved out! Phil went to his room and wept, sure that his bed-wetting had caused it all!

This kind of guilt can keep your grandchild feeling unworthy or unclean, and he may keep his distance from you.

Three is the strong sense of loyalty a child feels. Your grand-child may feel that overt movement toward you could be inter-preted to mean that he or she is taking sides with the parent who is your child. To risk losing either Mom or Dad is too frightening. Moving toward you might cause the other parent (your ex-law) to punish your child, your grandchild, or you.

Mrs. Wilkins was widowed, living comfortably in the downtown area of a large city. Her only son, Clyde, his wife, and two children lived out in the suburbs, and almost every week Clyde brought the children to her apartment. They loved the big-city excitement. Grandma and the kids sought a new adventure each visit. They went to the zoo, science museum, historic houses, special movies, and sang all the way there and back. Before their parents picked them up at the end of the day, they had feasted on Chinese food, spaghetti, or lobster. The whole visit was delicious for everyone.

One night Clyde called with the dismal news. He and his wife had separated. Before long, Mrs. Wilkins's son made a temporary move into a vacant apartment just above his mother's. His children stayed with their mother. Although they came to see Dad, they walked silently past Grandma's door. Clyde was too overwhelmed with his own miseries to talk to his children about their avoidance of their grandmother. After the divorce was final and the children settled, they told their dad about their fear that if they continued to see Grandma, it would be a betrayal of their mother. They were afraid of the questions Gram would ask. They thought silence was the way to protect both parents, that it was best not to show favoritism to one side of the family or the other.

Grandma, wisely patient, recognized and understood their behavior. She talked to Clyde about it but did not criticize him or them. She kept her door ajar when she knew they were visiting. One day, after many months, the children peeked in. Some weeks later, they pushed the door open, finally relaxed enough to resume their threesome, singing and all.

Four is the fear of abandonment. Your grandchild must hold tightly to both parents, not let them out of his sight, or one might disappear forever. It is common, after separation, for a young child to insist on sleeping with Dad, to follow either parent from room to room, to scream when Mom leaves for work, or to refuse to go to school. No one else will do for a while.

Some of the grandparents who talked to us became scapegoats, even demons, in the exploding accusations flung back and forth between their divorcers. When the grandchildren picked up on the themes and repeated the harsh words, the wounds went deep. "Dad says you caused all the trouble" is especially upsetting when it comes from young lips and you know the child believes it.

If your story has these overtones, your grandchildren may be looking for reasons for their catastrophe—or they could be just repeating the litany they have heard over and over at home. They are going through one of the most stressful periods of their lives. You probably can't stop the vituperation immediately, but you can set the record straight and calmly talk it over.

Let those grandchildren know that the decision to separate was their parents', not yours. Tell them that there is conflict in all married relationships. When differences outweigh satisfaction, couples retreat from each other, sometimes permanently. Keep it light. Don't give them more analysis than they can handle, but above all, be honest. Tell them, too, that you love them and are ready and willing to listen whenever they want an ear or a hug.

Of course, nothing you do will bring about a miraculous overnight change. For a quick fix, the sound of your voice or the music of your home will help. You are bedrock, and how you look and how you respond to your grandchild is crucial to your continuing connection. You need them and they need you.

The New Face of Holidays, Birthdays, and Gifts

The first holiday brings a new crisis. When the separation occurs just before Christmas or the Fourth of July picnic or granddaughter Betsy's fifth birthday, you have another hurdle to face, a change in your usual blueprint for celebrating. "We always got together on holidays. How will we face this? Couldn't they have waited until after the birthday to separate? Will our holidays turn into a holocaust?"

Family holidays mean far more than the day of celebration.

Planning begins months ahead; gifts to be bought, lots of talk about whose turn it is this year. Sometimes the other grandparents arranged the big birthday parties. Sometimes you did.

Now your pattern is changed and you have to change with it. You have to carry on, but it is unlikely that your ex-law will be with you. If he or she has custody of the children, the probability is that your grandchildren won't be sitting in their accustomed places some of the times, maybe all of them. If that happens to you, plan around your child's visitation days with your grandchildren—whether it is your birthday, Groundhog Day, or April Fool's Day. See if your child can negotiate for some of the holidays that are especially important to your family. If that doesn't work, fill in the empty places with your friends and your children's friends. You never know when your grandchildren may insist on coming back to your celebrations.

One defeated grandfather told us about the first Thanksgiving after his son's separation; his unhappiness was still apparent three years later:

> My wife and I are in semiretirement. I see patients just three days a week and she decided to limit her work to selling funds, instead of stocks and bonds, to schedule a three-day week for herself, too. My son and his wife are both trial lawyers and involved in political activity. With our reduced work schedule, we were always happy to pick up their three children instead of leaving them to the uncertain schedule of different sitters. We were all comfortable together. Holidays were always at our house since our daughter-in-law's family lives eight hundred miles away. Usually they spent some part of the summer vacation with the other grandparents and this seemed to work out just fine.
>
> Charles and Lily separated quite abruptly in October and she was fiercely bitter about another woman. The anger rolled on and, just before Thanksgiving, Charles told us that Lily was flying to Denver and the children were going along.
>
> Never in our lives have we spent so lonely and miserable a time as Thanksgiving 1981. We couldn't get ourselves together,

couldn't invite anyone else, and our own son couldn't face our wretchedness, so he stayed away, too.

Now our grandchildren live with their mother, in their original home, and although they visit us occasionally, our time together is brief, never relaxed. Perhaps the children blame us for our son's infidelity, which has caused such grief to their mother. Maybe we show too clearly that in some way we feel responsible for the broken home. We can't lift the cloud and the children sense it. Thanksgiving has never been the same at our house.

In another part of town, a grandmother of four swam with the tide, and although visits and holidays changed, they took on a new form:

Our daughter Louise was never going to remarry. When she and Sam separated (I'll never really know why), she slid easily into the singles' scene. She wasn't disgusted or angry, she just wanted to handle her life in her own way. Nothing was going to upset Louise again. She and my four grandchildren moved into a house that she could afford and they became part of a community of singles-with-children, who supported each other in lots of ways. There was no legal arrangement with Sam regarding support or visitation, but he was faithful about sending the monthly check and adjusted his schedule of visits with the children without trouble.

Sam has a big family and he asked if the children could spend both Thanksgiving and Christmas with them. Louise is our only child. The kids wanted to go because they thoroughly enjoy their fourteen cousins. Louise agreed. At first I was upset, but then I thought about the United States Congress and how they changed the date of Washington's Birthday and Lincoln's Birthday (I hated it at first but now it's fine with me; I'm used to it) with great ease and the celebrations take place on the new dates with just as much importance. If our Congress could take such action, so could I.

Thanksgiving in our house was to be celebrated eight days

after the official date and Christmas was a week ahead of time. The children loved the idea and bragged to their friends that this was to be a two-turkey Thanksgiving and Christmas meant two trees to trim and a load of extra presents.

We invited family and friends to our newly declared holidays and we all had a ball. Since the family had changed shape we felt that we could maneuver into a new flexible arrangement. We all loved it so much, we expect to repeat our holiday celebration on the dates we set next year.

Louise's mother was merely adapting to another stage in the evolution of her family. Freezing into one stage is unrealistic since all of life requires flexibility and change. This grand-mother creatively approached the challenge of the new shape of her family and found a solution that was innovative and seemed to work. The grandfather in the previous story allowed the separation, the divorce, and the remarriage to paralyze him into inactivity so that for many years afterward he wondered, "What-ever happened to Thanksgiving?"

Resorts in ski and palm-tree country have a system called time-sharing. You contribute to the purchase of a place but you live in it just one week of the year and the rest of the time it belongs to others. Your holidays, like these resort homes, might have to be "time-shared," but when it is your turn, make every moment count. Before the breakup, you might have had a proprietary right to every holiday; perhaps your family had closer ties than your in-law's family and a tradition of fine food, lively conversation, and an expectation that yours was the holiday home. Breakup time means another act is beginning; the program is likely to be very different. You will no longer take for granted every weekend, every Christmas, every birth-day, so you plan, discuss, and compromise, but continue your traditions.

Some grandchildren are the creative ones and plan a surprise, like the one related by this very pleased grandmother:

My granddaughters are eight and eleven years old. Their parents have been separated for two years and divorced just one month. Although they live with their mother, my ex-law, they come alone by bus, a distance of forty-five miles, each Friday after school to spend the weekend with my son. And each weekend, they spend some time with me in my home. We cook together, we visit the neighbors, and at times, when my son has a Saturday night something, they spend the night with me. My birthday was coming up, and although I prefer to just let it slip by, I thought the little ones should have a cakeful of candles to blow out and a chance to sing Happy Birthday. But I was the surprised one. They arrived that weekend with a large shopping bag crammed with birthday hats, a cake, candles, and a pin cushion handmade by the younger child and a little purse sewn by hand from the older one. Not only did they plan a surprise for me, but they included my sister, their great-aunt, and each child brought a special picture for her. This divorce certainly hasn't dimmed their enthusiasm, nor their creative talents. And they are as loving as ever.

When a breakup occurs, the combatants usually do not sit back and suggest to each other that since little Julie's birthday is just three weeks away, let's wait, have the party, and then resume our fight-to-the-end. Instead, your son moves out, and your daughter-in-law, about to become ex-law, is left with the battle-scarred house. Three weeks later, your ex-law buys a decorated birthday cake, pops the candles in it, and invites you and the other grandparents to the "party." Only your son is not invited. Every cell in your body wants to stay home, but somewhere in your mind a note is sounded that (a) the party will last only an hour and a half and you should be able to survive for that length of time, and (b) if ever little Julie needed the presence of some loving grandparents this is it. And you go.

You set forth with trepidation that meeting the other set of grandparents might be difficult. You might be angry at them, they at you. You could be furious with their child, they with yours. Yet, you all know that the first birthday without one parent is very hard on that eight-year-old. Think of her. This newly shocked child needs all the support she can get on this day of days. She may be threatened that her party could set the stage for a family fight. She may even have a sinking feeling that there will be fewer gifts for her to open than usual. She may fear that her school friends, guests, and cousins will sense that there is trouble in the air before she is ready to share her terrible news. She does not want her party spoiled! It is bad enough that Dad isn't there and probably won't be next year either or forever.

You will probably return from this first event on alien territory with every muscle sore, emotionally and physically exhausted. But you have passed the first test, and when other birthdays or school graduations occur, the terrible tensions of this first time around will have diminished. Your only alternative is to miss the pleasures you derive from these milestone experiences and to have your grandchild wonder why you are not at the party.

Gifts can be a problem. When you see the children less often you cannot always predict their passions. Mickey Mouse can become Sally the Alligator before a month has passed. When all the neighborhood kids are roller skating, a bike won't be appealing. When every shirt hangs out with big tails, one that is waist-length just won't do. If your grandchild is old enough to tell you what to send, ask directly. Otherwise, ask your child or the ex-law what would be most appreciated.

There are some disturbing aspects to playing Santa. Sometimes, if your ex-law is angry, he or she could prompt the children to ask for more expensive gifts than you can or want to give. Your ex-law could set you up to be a patsy. If you sense this, it is appropriate to tell your grandchild that you cannot afford a TV set, but would be glad to give him or her money to save for a future purchase.

On the other hand, you could on your own feel prompted to

give a more lavish gift than you would have given before the separation. You might even splurge to make up for the loss your grandchild is suffering or to lessen a lurking guilt that you might have contributed to the breakup. If you did not do so before, but feel now that you must present a gift every time you see your grandchild, think about that. Don't attempt to compete with the other set of grandparents. Setting up gift competition might cause your grandchildren to equate presents with love.

Creating New Ways to Keep in Touch

Many grandparents we interviewed spoke warmly about daily or weekly phone calls as a satisfying way to stay close. In many homes there is a Sunday-morning ritual of calling the kids immediately after picking up the paper and relaxing with a cup of coffee.

The sound of those young voices can hold you for the rest of the week, whether it travels through three states or just across town. Grandchildren know that you want to hear every word in their rambling sentences. If your ex-law has custody, these calls could be curtailed or prohibited. However, if these regular chats have been a ritual and you are not thwarted, keep them going. Don't use them to discuss either parent or to send angry messages. If you weren't in the habit of calling on a regular basis before the split-up and you suddenly start phoning, your grandchild might feel you are prying. If you can't telephone, try sending notes (printed for the younger ones), reminders, clippings, anything that says, "I'm thinking about you."

One grandfather whose grandson had moved four hundred miles away sends newsclippings that report on the football team in the new city, now home. A grandmother sends photos of Grandma and Granddad, or some that were taken of the family when they were all together. There are other devices. The Jarvises reported:

We really enjoy sending tapes to Rob and Ellie, our grandchildren. At first, it was audio only. We would tell them some news or a story and always how much we loved them. Last Christmas we gave them a VCR. Now we send videocassettes with both of us reciting a silly poem we made up just for them or a report on a trip we took.

They like sending messages to us, too. They are getting better at it all the time! Those voices are better than music for us! When we do get together on holidays we have shared experiences to talk about.

If you don't have cassettes and recorders, you can certainly send updated photos of yourselves and even of relatives who live nearby. If your grandchild is old enough to use it, sending an inexpensive camera and film can bring pictures back to you. Whenever you mail books, stickers, or jacket patches, you can include another roll of film.

Keeping in touch in a meaningful fashion does not necessarily require a big splash. The too-large, too-expensive stuffed elephant might be stashed in the basement because three-year-old Mikey took one look at it, burst into frightened sobs, and that was that. A racing car will just fit his little hand. Envelope stuffers like a sequined mask just before Halloween, a turkey sticker for the bedroom windows before you-know-when, a dollar bill for an eight-year-old, or a ten-dollar bill for a teen-ager can forge your links of understanding over and over. The springtime picture drawn with crayons that you tape to your refrigerator door is the delight of your heart—"my granddaughter sent it"—and the appropriate symbol you fold into an envelope is identified as "my grandma sent me this picture of a baby baboon and I love it." Keep the mail going—not every day, that's overkill, but every week or two; and wait until you find something that just fits your grandchild.

Remember, children can find addressing envelopes and locating stamps troublesome. If you send a stamped, self-addressed envelope in your packages, their picture, poem, or story has a better chance of reaching you.

Your Custody Battles, for Better and for Worse

In the early part of this century custody battles were big news. Gloria Vanderbilt's was one of those, set in giant type across the front pages of the newspapers. Her family name was a household word and staggering amounts of money were involved. In those years divorce was a privilege of the rich and famous and not the everyday occurrence it is now.

Your divorcers and their children could come out of the courtroom with many variations on the standard theme: Father gets custody (this is happening with more frequency). Mother gets custody; Father has the children every summer. Mother gets the kids all week, Dad on weekends, or vice versa. The parents split the week, four days here, three days there. Sometimes this is called "shared custody." In some cases, neither parent gets custody and, like the Vanderbilts, grandparents step in.

Family-court judges remove children from their parents only in special circumstances, such as physical abuse, emotional instability, addiction, or incarceration. When this is necessary, the court gives consideration to the desirability of close family members, including grandparents, or to a foster family.

Some grandparents take custody by default. "Our daughter was in a wheelchair and getting weaker," said Martha G. "And our son-in-law was an alcoholic. He beat the kids when he was drunk. We really didn't want to raise our six- and nine-year-old grandchildren, but we just couldn't consider the alternatives of foster care or adoption." This couple had misgivings, and when they accepted custody they became guardians for lack of a better alternative. Others go to court with a determination to fight for custody.

The courts take a dim view of grandparents as guardians and

often award grandchildren to foster parents instead. You wonder why. Judges state reasons of age and potentially deteriorat-
ing health. Can you envision yourself ten years down the road?
You are fifty-five or sixty-five and that dear little grandchild is
now a teenager. You are coping with a fifteen-year-old who is
experimenting with all sorts of clothing, new wave music, and
social relationships. Your energy level is not what it was when
you raised your own teenager. Now that your children are
grown and you have hindsight, you are less sure of your original
rules for rearing; and you are two generations removed from the
current youth culture. A few of the grandparents we spoke with
were perfectly well when they took custody but quite ill ten
years later. One had a stroke and her mate had a heart attack;
one had a quadruple heart bypass and her husband had a leg
amputation. None of them could state decisively whether they
were doing right by raising their grandchildren.

Remember that your grandchildren have probably had unusual difficulties in their young lives or the court would not
consider removing them from their home. As they grow up,
their emotional needs will be greater than those of the average
child. This is one of the many issues to consider if you want
custody.

If you are married, the strength of your relationship with your
mate is another consideration. Several older couples we spoke
with had barely survived the empty nest. At first, the grandchildren they took in appeared to stabilize their relationship, to
fill their home with renewed life. Down the road, the additional strains of ailing health and troubled teenagers were more
than their marriage could bear. While they made it with difficulty through the rearing of their own children, handling the
challenge of live-in grandchildren was too much. One over-
loaded grandfather walked out; one grandmother moved to the
Sun Belt in response to Grandpa's interference. "He under-
mined my discipline with our children. He's not going to
undermine it now."

By comparison, there were some good, solid couples—like the

A.s—who worked together in tandem. She was in charge of meals, he of bedtime. They were careful to continue their nights out at the theater, their friendships, and their vacations alone together. They would have liked to move to a retirement community at this stage of their lives, but they agreed they would feel too guilty. The A.s settled for semiretirement and he pitched in with both grandchildren. We last saw Nana with one of the youngsters on a fair-housing picket line.

At your age, it is best if there are other relatives nearby who are interested and involved. It helps to have other children and grandchildren in the neighborhood to take your young ones along to school or to Girl Scouts and Little League. A favorite aunt or another set of grandparents can extend invitations for overnights and weekends, a welcome time off for you. Count your helping hands when you size up the custody issue. Even the best of modern families are hard-pressed for lack of nearby, concerned relatives.

A final consideration is money. Those of you with enough money can hire a housekeeper or send your grandchildren to private school. However, if money is tight in your household, you won't have the dependable seventh-inning stretch, giving you time to relax your vigil and better prepare for the coming storms. Overfatigue affects your tolerance level as well as your muscle tone. Money can most assuredly ease many of the tight spots for grandparents who take over twenty-four-hour duty as parents.

Custody is an issue of concern to only a minority of grandparents and grandchildren, but, with the proliferation of divorce, it occurs often enough to bear mention. There are the options of a foster home or adoption. Although we have emphasized the hazards of taking responsibility for your grandchildren, we think that a foster home takes last place. While there are excellent foster homes and good adoptions, we know of grandchildren who ran off to grandparents who wanted custody in the first place.

A No Visitation Sign on the Door

For most grandparents the important question about custody is who walks out of the courtroom with the children, your child or ex-law. No matter who wins, even if custody is shared, you may be left with a gnawing uneasiness that your grandchildren will be short-changed. You will probably be more involved if your child gets custody. There's no guarantee that consequently everything will run smoothly for you, but the chances are better that they will. If your ex-law wins the battle, you may be in for quite a tug-of-war.

If ever there was a time to watch what you say, this is it, because a powerful command can be leveled at you: "Keep away from my children, your grandchildren!" Most grandparents continue to have access to their grandchildren, but the number of those being exiled grows. Frequently this can be traced to a poor relationship prior to the separation. There are grandparents whose contacts with their in-law during the marriage were so poor, so replete with friction, criticism, and harsh words, that immediately following the divorce the in-law considers herself divorced from her in-laws, too. Even when the relationship was good, grandchildren are not permitted to see grandparents and are hardened against them due to misunderstandings, misconceptions, or misplaced anger. A No Visitation sign on the door has become common enough to warrant recent legislation for grandparents' visitation rights on a state and national level.

Only four states had visitation laws prior to 1980; now all states have them. However, the present system has severe drawbacks. If grandparents win their rights in one state and their grandchildren are moved to another, they have to renew their appeal and start afresh. It is this situation that prompted Congress to pass a Model Visitation Statute which they hope each state will adopt.

Even if the law becomes uniform across the country, it still does not guarantee automatic access to your grandchildren. The burden of proof remains on you to show why you should be able to see them and that it is in their best interests to see you. Parents take the initial action when they banish you. They do not have to prove why you are unworthy and should not be allowed to visit with, indulge, and enjoy your grandchildren. A model law on the federal level is not ideal, but it offers hope for those of you who are determined to fight in the courts.

Although you who are renounced are a small group, your agonies cannot be ignored. You want to keep the lines of communication open, and if your ex-law has custody you have to go through him or her unless your child has the foresight to ask that your access be included in the divorce agreement. If there is a Keep Out sign on the door, you are locked out. If your child has left the scene or is dead, your only hope to see your grandchildren is the ex-law route. Even if he or she allows you to see them sometimes, his or her case against you may be reviewed daily with the children. They may hear you vilified with a steady stream of anger at your omissions or commissions, true or untrue. In some cases the ex-law is so determined to color you unfit that he or she lies unmercifully. Some angry divorcers we heard about went to the extreme of unjustifiably accusing grandparents of alcoholism or molestation of their grandchildren. Should this happen to you, you can clear yourselves at great personal and financial cost, but your grandchildren might have heard all of the character assassination and reject you on the basis of it.

Sometimes, even when your own child has custody, because of grief or anger he could cut off all contact and refuse you visitation rights. These quarantined children grow up without your affectionate attention and you are denied loving contact with them.

What can you do to avoid being a victim of your child's divorce?

1. When your child is negotiating the divorce, ask him to include requests for your rights, too. Your inherent privilege can be part of the settlement if your divorcer is willing to ask

the lawyer to fight for it. It is up to you to initiate and press for your right to see your grandchild. Your child, caught up in his or her own troubles, may not want to bother about your interests. Try to be persuasive and insistent. Explain how much your grandchildren mean to you. You should do this even if your child has custody, for if he or she should die, your ex-law will become custodian and then there could be more trouble.

2. If your ex-law interferes with your contacts with the grandchildren, avoid becoming an adversary. Do everything you can to communicate with him or her. If direct contact is out of the question, ask relatives, friends, religious leaders, mental health professionals, doctors, lawyers, or mediators to intercede.

3. Start or join a chapter of the Grandparents/Children's Rights organization. This organization has contact leaders in at least thirty-five states and is rapidly growing. Leaders offer much information by telephone and mail and often organize lobbying efforts on behalf of grandparents. They are a good ear for your troubles and a good source of advice. To find your nearest contact leader, write:

> Lee and Lucile Sumpter
> Box 444
> Hazlett, MI 48840

4. Join a support group. Discussion with other grandparents experiencing the same loss can rescue you from drowning. You can talk freely there. They understand your frustration and can offer the benefit of their experiences. Being surrounded by those who share your grief and pain is usually helpful. Sources for information about counseling and support groups are:

> Scarsdale Family Counseling Service
> 403 Harwood Building
> Scarsdale, NY 10583

> The Foundation for Grandparenting
> P.O. Box A, Rte 86
> Jay, NY 12941

5. Court captures headlines and court sets precedents, but it is a place of last resort. Courts cannot legislate a relationship. Once you go before a judge, you are in an out-and-out power struggle, and you can lose sight of the best interests of your grandchildren. Remember, they have been through battles and conflicts of loyalty with their parents, and a court case involving you will add to the stress and havoc in their young lives. You have to weigh this against the importance of letting them know you care enough to fight to see them.

Those who have been to court say it is very costly, both financially and emotionally. The wear and tear often result in physical symptoms as well. Occasionally there is an early decision that settles the matter, but it is more the rule that both parties become increasingly adversarial. It is often necessary to go through investigations by a court-appointed officer.

Psychiatric examinations, hearings and appeals, and lawyers' fees can run as high as $60,000 (the highest reported to us). Recent decisions have run more in favor of grandparents than not. Some grandparents have petitioned the family court, have gained access without having a lawyer, and the judge did grant them visitation rights.

The Laytons, in upstate New York, had incredible luck along with their determination. Their grandson was adopted by his stepfather after their daughter-in-law remarried and their son gave up rights to his child. When they were barred from seeing him, they decided to go to court. They knew that in previous cases of adoption the courts had ruled against the rights of natural grandparents, but they were attached to that boy. They had taken care of him for a few years and they could not accept their tragic fate. They lost the first round in court, but the judge was sympathetic enough to connect them with a lawyer who pursued their interests further. That lawyer worked gratuitously and won their case for them, and today they have the pleasure of periodic visits with their nine-year-old grandchild.[4]

That case provided hope for other grandparents in other states, especially because those grandparents invoked the Grandparents' Visitation Act without the aid of their own son and because their grandson's mother and new father did honor the court decision. There are other parents who do not honor court decisions, such as the hostile ex-law who used excuses from high fever to grounded planes to sabotage the visits.

When grandparents are awarded visitation rights, sometimes specific restrictions are imposed: (1) visits are directed to take place at a certain location, for instance in a restaurant in the town where the grandchildren reside; (2) there may have to be a legal guardian or court-appointed overseer present during the visits.

The M.s found that their court victory created new tensions:

We were thrilled when the judge found in favor of visitation for us once every seven weeks. Seven times a year was better than being cut off forever from Rob and Lisbeth. The big "but" was we had to visit them in their home, in the presence of their mother, who had taken them to live with her parents. We figured we could live with that; we wanted to continue a relationship with their mother, Sally, anyway. But when we went there, her whole clan was present. It was humiliating. We all sat around in the living room watching the children play in the center, like it was a cockfight. I motioned for the little one, Rob, to come, I had a toy for him. Instead, he ran to his mother and clung to her leg, staring at me. She appeared to be stroking him but I could see—we could all see—she was holding him back.

The visits got more and more stressful. Every time one was due we would get a phone call. "Lisbeth has a birthday party she wants to go to. . . . We have a christening." All kinds of obstacles, postponements, and trade-offs. It got so we stopped marking off days on the calendar. The disappointments were too great.

After a few months, we felt our grandchildren were dreading the visits. They never kissed us when we came, and kept their distance. The family never gave us the courtesy of seeing them alone and we felt miserably rejected. After a while we gave up. Somebody in my support group told us, "A man doesn't fail. He just gives up." That's us. We just gave up and thanked God we had other grandchildren to enjoy.

Courtrooms are frequently arenas for revelations, truths and lies, confrontation and conflict. Suits are costly and the outcome unforeseeable and unpleasant. Sometimes grandparents, like the M.s, give up and, if they don't have other grandchildren, become foster grandparents to those who are more appreciative. Sometimes grandparents do nothing and, after a period of heartbreak, their grandchildren insist on making their own decisions to see them; the closeness is reborn.

The best prevention against being denied access, if it is not too late, is to keep the lines with your in-law and your grandchildren open, warm, connected. When the in-law becomes ex-law, don't denigrate him or her. Handle your family relationships at this crucial time with as much tact as you can. It could pay off in gratifying ways, prevent retribution, and keep those grandchildren close to you.

Some Silent Anxieties

1. Are your grandchildren branded by divorce?
In the past, a child of divorce was alone and often felt disgraced. Families stayed together, burying deep their secrets of adultery, alcoholism, wife beating, and the bad chemistry between husband and wife. They appeared a united front at church and at family celebrations. The children carried the heavy burden of secrecy and joined Mom and Dad in the big lie of a happy family. When a couple divorced, the family was stigmatized. Their child might have been the only one in the classroom whose mother and father sat apart on Parents' Night.

Today, your grandchildren may feel self-conscious when their parents decide to separate. It means telling friends some disturbing stories about how life is at their home. It means their schoolwork will probably suffer and their class participation diminish. Just as with adults, however, after a while your grandchild will realize that his situation is not unique, that there are lots of others in his fix. In some schools nowadays, the children of intact families are in a minority.

The setting is a fairly small, traditional private school in a large, metropolitan area. The school is conservative in that the children must be properly attired, they move from classroom to classroom in orderly, quiet fashion, and the teaching staff stands at the head of the class attired in jacket and tie (men) and skirt (not pants) for the women. But the children are approached as individuals and the educational achievement level is high.

Staff and administration recognize that a high percentage of the students lived in "broken" homes and meetings for parents were rarely attended by both parents.

An evening was planned for single parents only. In a fourth-grade class, everyone was talking about it except one little boy, Jason. He was the only one in that class of fourteen children whose parents were still married and still living together.

When he went home the day of the singles' meeting, he opened the front door to hear a family argument in progress and waited until there was a pause in the angry shouting. "Wow! Are you going to get a divorce?" he asked eagerly, feeling he was the only one in his class whose parents wouldn't be at school tonight.

2. Will they come home from school to an empty house?

They call them latch-key children and you are distraught at the idea that your grandchild is one. For some children this is a positive experience. They achieve early independence of thought, decision, and discipline. Responsibility forces them into self-reliance at an earlier age than was required of your children, who were probably more closely supervised.

Remember that daily movements in and out of households have changed considerably since you raised your children. The percentage of working mothers with preschool-age children jumped from 34 percent in 1967 to 55 percent in 1981. Babies

as young as three months old are left at infant-care centers until
Mom or Dad picks them up after work. Some fathers, whose
own fathers and grandfathers never went into the kitchen, now
are recognized as the best bread-bakers among all their friends,
and their young sons produce the spiciest chili. Junior is not
suddenly confronted with household chores at divorce time; he
may have been doing them all along. Some grade-school children have keys to the front door, take the dog for a walk as
soon as they arrive home after school, defrost a casserole, and
begin their homework without reminders from parents. It's
routine. A recent child-care study of third-graders in a Dallas
suburb showed that youngsters who returned to a home without
a parent did as well as those whose parent was at home.[5]

Most likely your daughter or daughter-in-law didn't start to
work outside the home at the point of breakup. She has been
working all along. Your generation was more likely to begin
new routines when a separation occurred. Mom always obtained
custody of the kids and then frequently had to go to work. She
had to tell the children that now they would have to be
responsible for themselves after school and accept dishwashing
and Saturday clean-up as regular procedures. Now, 11 million
children in the United States have no child care while both
parents work. Since both Dad and Mom are not home, their
phone numbers are posted on the kitchen bulletin board. Sometimes the children are told to phone as soon as they come home
from school; others, only to phone if there's an emergency.

Most aspects of family life have changed. Children watch TV
shows depicting family arguments, sex, separation, divorce,
stepparents, and how a bunch of little kids move with their
dad into the home of a bunch of little kids with their mom and
what fun they have. The specter of the wicked stepmother has
moved far down the scale because little Bernice has three
friends in her class who live with stepmothers and dinners at
their houses are just great.

Even in unbroken homes, when Junior awakens with a raw
throat, fever, and the need for tender loving care, he is more

than likely left in bed for the day with lots of Coke and orange juice nearby and instructions about not too much TV, stereo, Walkman, or computer. Doctors no longer make housecalls, and parents no longer take time off from work when their children are sick. Junior is phoned several times during the day to find out how he is doing, but dual careers and the necessity for two incomes require early independence on the part of the children.

For some children, being left to their own devices and discipline is disaster. They are afloat for several hours each day and can't settle down to doing homework when there is no one to say, "Turn off the TV," or, "Take an apple or a glass of milk instead of nachos and a Coke." Their problems are fairly universal and alarming. To help them, you could offer to have your grandchildren come to your home occasionally or on a regular basis. The shared time gives you the opportunity to see them one to one, and to help out your child or ex-law.

3. *Will they see a succession of sexual partners parading through their parent's home?*

There's a good chance your grandchildren will learn a lot more about dating and mating than you think they should, no different from the sexy messages they have already gotten from watching TV. Under their new living arrangements they are going to be upset and jealous when either parent goes on a date, no matter how young or old they are. Seeing Mom or Dad with another man or woman brings up feelings of suspicion, longing for the security of two live-in parents, and fear that this "date" may become a permanent fixture in their precarious home. Often your child or your ex-law does settle into a long-lasting relationship at some point, even immediately. Whether it is a succession of partners, a steady visitor, or a live-in, the young ones are watching closely, learning a lot.

Many grandparents we spoke with had a subtle fear of their child's promiscuity following the divorce. Sons were going to play the field and make up for lost time, while daughters might get lonely and desperate enough to jump in and out of the sack indiscriminately. Clearly, your grandchildren will figure out that their parents are not monogamous. There is no reason to believe that divorcers are any more exhibitionistic or less discreet about their sex than they were during marriage.

Some of your children are as concerned as you are about what your grandchildren see and know. This was evident in our interviews with divorced couples, although there was an interesting difference in the sexual patterns of custodial mothers and noncustodial fathers. If the latter had a live-in girlfriend, the couple tended to sleep together during the weekend visits of the children. Some mothers with boyfriends often had them sleep in separate rooms if they stayed the night. Other mothers brought a lover to the house only when the children were away, usually overnight at Daddy's. As one woman explained, "In front of my children, it's still a matter of morality. Do I think it's wrong? Not exactly. But I know they're watching, they might ask questions, and I don't like my sex life being so public." Those children, your grandchildren, can be an exacting public.

They will probably know what's happening in their parents' love lives before you do, so be prepared. When you are together they may suddenly mention a new name in their chatter. You may be talking to them on the phone and casually learn that a new person tucked them in last night, or that somebody named Janie fixed their oatmeal this morning. These are the first signs of Spring and, unwittingly, your grandchild may be the harbinger. He or she is accepting it, but you are startled. Your curiosity may itch, your tongue bristle with a thousand questions. Try to save them for your son or daughter. Don't pump your grandchild.

Where Do You Get on the Shuttle?

Being a grandparent is different after divorce from what it was before. If your child has custody, you will see the children more often, do more baby-sitting, get more involved in bringing clothes and toys. Your chances for spontaneous visits are greater when the grandchildren live nearby. Long-distance meetings are less frequent of necessity, and need more planning, but these reunions can be packed with enjoyment and love. Even when your ex-law has custody and lives a distance from you, if your own child approves and you are welcome, visits to that home can be a happy gathering. It is important to go in their direction sometimes. Many grandchildren want you to meet their new friends, see where they now live, and what their new school looks like.

See those grandchildren you must, if you love the way they flesh out your life, and if you cannot give up the idea that they are your hope for continuity. They give you the chance to watch and feel the agonies and ecstasies, the stages of growing up from smooth-bottomed baby to uncertain adolescent. You have the right to see the future as it rolls in.

It is not a one-way street. They need you, too, for stability, special devotion, and the sense that they have traditions and relatives who accept and love them. Without this, your grandchildren will grow up with a deep and recurrent sadness inside them, as evidenced by this young mother:

I am thirty-one years old, separated, and the mother of four children. I am also the product of a broken home. During my childhood, I had very little family contact, no real relationships with grandparents, aunts, uncles, or cousins. Holidays were meager in my family. Did you ever eat turkey on an empty feeling?

To this day, I experience a very deep loss, a sense of being cheated or deprived. You see, I knew these members of my family existed, but was never encouraged to see them or to develop any relationships with them.

Just a month ago, an aunt of mine came to town. Her daughter is friendly with my best friend and I happened to drop in to say hello. Can you imagine how unimportant I felt running into my aunt and cousin that way? Here I am, their blood relation, and it would never occur to them to call me when they came to town.

For this very reason, I find it necessary and most important to see that my children stay in touch with their families, meaning the grandparents, aunts, uncles, and cousins from their father's side as well as mine. I love to hear their excitement after an ice cream with Aunt Mary and Uncle Joe, or a trip to Great Adventure with their grandparents. I listen to their babble and, believe me, I drink it all up.

Imagine not knowing what it is like to have special days with Grandpa. I didn't. Other children had a favorite aunt or a best cousin to do things with. Not me. In a way, I would have felt less cheated if my relatives didn't exist. But all that potential was there and I never got to taste it.

We, as parents, don't always realize that when we deprive our children of these experiences for any number of reasons, we harm them emotionally. When two people divorce or separate, innocent people can be crippled by our decisions. We may want to hurt ex-relatives by staying out of touch, but we scar our children more.

When couples divide, let the love of relatives multiply.

—Barbara Ruggeri[6]

1. The Relationship with Grandparents: Contact, Importance, Role Conception. Timothy S. Hartshorne, Wichita State University, and Guy J. Manaster, The University of Texas at Austin. *International Journal of Aging & Human Development* v. 15, no. 3, 1982, pp. 233–245.

2. Kornhaber, Arthur, M.D., and Kenneth Woodward, *Grandparents/Grandchildren: The Vital Connection* (Anchor Press/Doubleday, 1981).

3. Wallerstein, Judith, and Jean Kelly.

4. Greene, Jill Rothfeld, "They Said We'd Never See Our Grandson Again," *McCall's*, September 1984.

5. Swan, Helen L., and Victoria Houston, *Alone After School*, A Guide for Kids and Families (Prentice-Hall, 1984).

6. *The New York Times*, Westchester Section, Letter to the Editor, June 9, 1985.

9

Disturbing Disclosures

When Your Divorcer Comes Out of the Closet

INTERVIEWER: When did you discover Gary was homosexual?

HENRY: That was one of the problems; Gary came to us and told us about the divorce himself. He told us he was moving out and going to live with a friend, and we weren't happy but we thought it sounded okay. It sounded economical and transitional and not too drastic a step in case he changed his mind. It took us a while to put two and two together.

CHRISTINA: Two and two or one and one? (laughter) You forget it was really Carol who made us see it.

HENRY: That's right. It was that talk we had with his wife. She knew about it when they got married but she married him anyway. She was more prepared for it than we were, angry that we were so blind.

CHRISTINA: It was hard for her in a different way. I know I'm not supposed to feel this way, but I'm sorry for her. I feel as though I pushed Gary into marrying her by being so enthusiastic.

There were many things that were hard for this couple to get used to. Henry's image of homosexuals was old-fashioned and stereotyped. It meant feminine gestures and sibilant speech and it was impossible for him to fathom that this handsome, professional son of his could be gay. For a long time he denied it, saying it was just a phase, and reminisced aloud about all the girls Gary used to date. His homophobia made him doubt his own virility and his image of himself as a strong father figure. Fantasies interfered with his own sexuality for many months.

Christina shared her husband's stereotype and worried about her own as well. Was she the overbearing mother who had created a gay son? Ultimately, the couple went to Gary's therapist with him and were helped to discuss their feelings and questions more openly. Gary reassured his mother that, although he had his gripes, her tyranny was not one of them. He felt he had had a strong chemical reaction to males as far back as when he was eight years old, in addition to which he by no means hated women. More than anything, what he wanted now from his parents was their acceptance of his lover into the family, but it took them more than a year to invite Bob to their home.

No matter how modern and open-minded you are about homosexuality—recognizing that it's not a crime or an illness, that it has a physiological basis—if you discover that a major cause of your child's divorce is that he's gay or she's lesbian, it is difficult to comprehend. As one parent described it, "It's as though all your life you were sure you knew that what you saw was the color green and suddenly you are asked to believe it is red."

You will go over and over your divorcer's childhood with a new and jaundiced eye, looking for clues you might have noticed and dismissed. You will wonder what part you played in the development of his or her sexuality. You will be alarmed about AIDS.

If friends and family ask you the reasons for your child's divorce, what will you answer? If you are as uncomfortable as some parents we interviewed, you will become an expert in vagueness and understatement. According to Dr. Barbara Rothberg, Brooklyn family therapist, the biggest problem for you may be dealing with your peer group. "They decided they were incompatible," you might offer without amplification, or, "They weren't happy as a couple."

Stella and Nathan Gross used a family picture to announce their daughter's relationship. This couple has five grown children and lots of money. There has always been a healthy balance in their home between luxury and responsibility. When the children were younger the whole family went on trips into the sun during winter holidays. At home, the kids were expected to push the lawn mower, shovel the snow, and take out the trash.

Child number three, Winnie, had married her high-school sweetheart, settled nearby, and had two children. The marriage was what social workers call uneventful. After their eighth anniversary, Winnie left her husband and children to move from the suburbs into a downtown studio apartment with her lover, a woman. The parents had no inkling that their daughter was lesbian and even more could not conceive that she would desert her children. They were sophisticated enough to tolerate an affair, but a lesbian affair combined with child desertion was incomprehensible. The immediate response was to join forces with their son-in-law and grandchildren. They hardly saw their daughter. As the months passed and summertime approached, Nathan and Stella invited Winnie to join them for a weekend in the mountains at the same time her children were visiting. They missed her and hoped for a reunion with the children. Winnie accepted on the condition that her lover could join them. Stella and Nathan steeled themselves and said yes.

Three years later, on Thanksgiving, the latest family photo on the wall included all of Stella and Nathan's children, their wives and husbands, the grandchildren, and, standing beside Winnie, her female companion. The Grosses had kept their family intact.

By contrast, one deeply religious Jewish family observed the traditional mourning ceremony of shiva when they learned that their son was homosexual and thereafter considered him dead.

When your grandchildren live in a homosexual household, you may be alarmed at what they will sense in the bedroom. (1) Will they grow up with doubts about their own sexuality? (There is no proof one way or the other.) But for your grandchildren sexuality will be a more sensitive issue because their parent is different from many of their friends' parents. All children go through a long period when they worry about their own sexual identity. In addition to normal anxieties, your grandchildren may fear that they have inherited a same-sex preference. The nature of their inner conflict depends on how much they identify with the homosexual parent. (2) Will they feel different in school? (Probably yes, by a certain age.) In adolescence, when feeling different is especially unacceptable, your grandchild may want to hide the fact that he or she lives in a homosexual home. At that time the teenager may feel squeamish about a parent's appearance at school or about inviting friends home. However, this phase of wanting to be like everybody else can be weathered as successfully as the other conflicts connected with adolescence.

Before talking about homosexuality with your grandchildren, you may want to know what their parents have explained. Recognize your own attitude and how that affects them. You can give them a perspective by providing—but not pushing—an alternate role model. In homosexual as in heterosexual households, the day-to-day quality of the relationships, the stability, and the nurturance offered the children are more significant than what goes on behind the bedroom door.

Custody is a serious issue, since in contested cases the courts usually award children to the heterosexual parent, regardless of his or her other qualities. Sometimes joint custody is a solution, and in that case you don't have to worry that your access to the children will be at risk. All these anxieties crowd in on you when you are still reeling from trying to accept the sexual preference of your child.

Homosexuality and the fear of AIDS are today almost inseparable. You may be alarmed that your child could be a carrier or a victim, that your grandchildren could be infected through ordinary daily contact, or that you yourself could become infected. Some of the data regarding the deadly virus are known, but medical science has not yet uncovered a cure. Nor are all the facts regarding its transmission understood. The current information is:

1. Tests for AIDS-infected people, both carriers and the afflicted, are available.
2. AIDS is transmitted through sexual activity, the use of second-hand needles by intravenous drug takers, or from improperly tested blood used during a transfusion.
3. An AIDS victim will *not* transmit the disease to you or to anyone else during the normal routine of living together.

Since new research on AIDS is reported frequently, update your concerns with a knowledgeable physician.

Learning all you can about homosexuality will be very helpful to you. Much of the emotional baggage you carry in your head is outdated, fraught with old wives' tales and the biblical view of sodomy. Not too long ago the American Psychiatric Society removed homosexuality from its list of illnesses and now perceives it as an alternative form of normal human sexual expression. The vote for removal reflected the clinical observations of psychiatrists who had been treating homosexuals.

If you cannot stop the merry-go-round of thoughts that run through your head about things in the past you could have, should have done differently, you can seek information and understanding through a support group in your area. The director of your local human-services agency can give you specifics. Some such groups are listed as Parents and Friends of Lesbians and Gays. You can find relief and enlightenment in such sessions. If you attend, instead of feeling that you alone are a persecuted parent you will find a roomful of doctors, lawyers, policemen, clerks, and housewives, parents all. (A full 10 percent of the population of this country is homosexual.) They will exchange views on the coping mechanism they have used to help them over the first troubled period through the time when the news spread from the confines of their families and became general knowledge. One thing you all share is that your image of an ideal family is shattered. Other parents of divorcers can hope that their child will remarry, but a new in-law child or more grandchildren from your gay or lesbian child is unlikely. Yet you may find, as many have, that a homosexual relationship can grow into a new kind of family with loyalty, stability, shared interests, and love.

Alcoholism

Ethel and Arthur Metz had an only child, Bill, who married someone they liked very much. They gave the couple a big check to give them a good start and then sat back to enjoy the marriage. One year later, Bill returned with his suitcase and furniture and announced that he was not staying in the marriage. The rest is Ethel's version of the story:

> I was furious. I really cried for six months because I took that daughter-in-law into my heart like she was mine. So did Art. Bill said she drinks and he didn't want to be married to an alcoholic, and I said, "Alcoholic? Because she drinks at parties? Everybody does that." He insisted she drank at home and I said, "Everybody drinks a cocktail before dinner." I didn't know she had accused Bill's best friend of raping her while she was high. It was a while before he told us that part, but even then I felt he should at least give her a second chance. I really felt he gave up too quickly and that maybe she would join AA or something like that.
>
> The problem was that we never actually saw his wife drunk, so it was hard to believe. He may have been living with the situation for a year but it was news to us. It might've been easier if we'd had some inkling along the way or if we hadn't liked her, but I remember saying to Bill, "She's always been so nice to us." It was a selfish thing to say, but it was hard for us to understand.

Dependence on alcohol is woven into the warp and woof of our society. It is the most frequently accepted and excused addiction not only in America but in many other countries. One young man told us that when he would go out and get high on drugs he would then stop at a bar on the way to visit his parents so that they would think he was drunk on liquor. That seemed okay to them, manly, macho, and legal. Many families silently cope with alcoholism and its excesses even when it produces frightening results, i.e., uncontrolled anger, abuse, job loss. Employers often give second and third chances to alcoholics. Too often our courts excuse drunken drivers who commit murder on the streets.

The drinking of alcoholic beverages is part of celebrations in most cultures of the world. Whether the brew is beer, liquor, or wine, celebrants become merrier or more hostile, looser of limb or totally rigid. There is rarely a problem with moderate drinking, but when alcohol dominates everyday existence it fits the medical diagnosis of addictive disease. Heavy drinking affects the liver, nervous system, and eventually the processes of the brain. More families have histories and points of reference in relation to alcoholism than to any other disturbance that might emerge at separation and divorce time.

Alcoholics Anonymous (AA) brought the subject of this addiction to public awareness and provided peer group friendship and pressure. AA provides support for the alcoholic and for his or her family. A high percentage of individuals who go the AA route and stay with it have remained sober for long periods. Recently the plight of the families of alcoholics has been recognized and given considerable support by Alcoholics Anonymous in groups such as Alateen for children of problem drinkers and Al-Anon for their spouses. There is also Teen Challenge for children over eighteen years who may have trouble coping with a parent drunk and out of control. The children of alcoholics are at risk for future alcoholism. But scaring these children will be counter-productive. The best thing grandparents can do is to serve as models of responsibility.

A relatively recent movement is the "intervention" process. When families recognize alcoholism in a member, they agree collectively to persuade him or her lovingly but firmly to enter treatment before the disease destroys everyone. After preparation by a counselor, they gather together without the drinker's prior knowledge to confront him or her with honest statements about how the lack of dependability, irresponsible behavior, money problems or brutality affect them.

Intervention counselors stress that the very process of dealing with alcoholism openly as a family is healthy in itself. It can save other family members even if the alcoholic refuses treatment. Denial on the part of the drinker as well as the rest of the family is often the central problem.

Drugs

Few people today are addicted only to alcohol. They often have additional dependence on prescription or illegal drugs. Anxiety over dependence on drugs has become one of the most exploited fears in the 1980s. The words *meth, crack,* and *coke* send tremors through us all. When parents find their child is heavily addicted to the expensive hard stuff they are in panic and often irrational. If your drug-dependent son or daughter runs home to you from his or her marriage, you have to confront the tragedy and face what your in-law child probably knows too well.

Phil and Denise Bryant are parents who now admit they initially responded exactly the wrong way. Middle-aged, blue-collar, they live in a mortgage-free home on a tree-shaded street. They have four children, three of whom are sons. Child number four is a daughter, Sherry, who was always her father's favorite. When she married, Phil could not control his sobs as he walked his daughter down the aisle. Sherry is petite and pretty and indulged by her brothers as well as her father. Denise tried to force her daughter to study (she was an indifferent student), to keep her room neat, and to be considerate about playing her stereo, but Phil always excused her failures because she was "so young" ("She'll grow up soon enough"), and Denise was shamed into silence.

When Sherry flounced home announcing she couldn't take her husband anymore, her mother sensed that she was high on drugs. Denise found herself unable to tell her daughter what she suspected or to share the suspicion with her husband, who wouldn't have believed it anyway. Denise hid other incriminating facts: her jewelry had gradually disappeared, and the family silver tea set was taken from the buffet, piece by piece.

Phil gave his daughter an allowance, which she used to buy cocaine. Although Denise urged her to get a job, Sherry never got around to it. Phil and Denise were fighting daily because they disagreed about how Sherry was to be treated. When one of Sherry's brothers came home for a visit, he detected that she was heavily addicted and insisted that his parents do something about it. Denise wanted to have her admitted to a hospital for detoxification, but Phil held out for an outpatient methadone clinic. Phil won, and after three months he and his wife were called by the police. Sherry had been arrested for attempted robbery—mugging an old woman on the street.

The court process was deeply humiliating but forced both parents to unite in their efforts to help their daughter. Given the choice by the judge, Sherry chose to live in a drug-free community rather than jail. Her husband washed his hands of her completely and would not participate in any efforts to make her drug-free, but her parents joined the mandatory group for families of drug abusers connected with her program. When Sherry came home for an occasional weekend and went out for the evening, she was fully aware that her parents would call the probation officer if she was not home by ten o'clock. It seemed that their willingness to agree on setting limits, reinforced by group pressure and the judge's backup, helped Sherry grow up. Phil and Denise had sidestepped the early danger signals of her immaturity, her failed marriage, and her drug addiction. Only when she became involved with the criminal justice system did they stand together and decide to help save her.

Abuse

If you discover that your divorcing child has been a wife, husband, or child abuser, it is important that he or she get professional help as quickly as possible from a therapist and a local group for spouse/child abusers. Convincing him or her to do so is often not easy. Most people who mistreat others do not own up to their illness. It's always somebody else's fault, not his or her problem. It will be to everyone's benefit if you can convince your child that he or she can change with the help of a counselor. If you cannot persuade him or her by argument, you may have to get tough, shut your door, and take the stand that you will joyfully open it when your son or daughter faces facts and starts therapeutic treatment. You may get a real backup for your position from the judge in the divorce court. Many judges now prescribe and insist on therapy for abusers and impose harsh penalties for noncompliance.

When your child stays with an abusive spouse for many years, you have a different set of problems. Once you understand what your child has been exposed to for so long, you ask yourself why she put up with it. You wonder if you did something wrong when you raised her. One set of parents felt guilty because their daughter had been mistreated for many years and had been elusive about her bruises and scratches. When they questioned her, she answered, "Oh, I burned myself on the iron," or "The cat was impossible last night," and the matter was dropped. They forgot about it. This couple became enraged when they learned the truth, and they not only embraced their child's divorce, they insisted on it. In spite of their pleading, however, their daughter returned to her husband, and they no longer speak to her. They are angry and in pain, but they insist that she can always come home if she leaves him. They "will do anything to get rid of Frankenstein."

Insisting on their daughter's divorce and not speaking to her when she returned to her husband are understandable, but they are not measures we recommend. You may have difficulty trusting your child's judgment if she has stayed in a destructive relationship, but your taking over or backing out completely are reactions, not solutions, to the problem.

If your child is married to Trouble for a long time and is finally trying to get out of it, she may know better than you do what ropes are available to save her. Some mates of abusers know about calling the police, obtaining an order of protection from family court, and going to an emergency shelter. But many do not. Don't be surprised if it takes your child more than one attempt to leave. One problem may be that her husband has given her an ultimatum that if she goes home to her parents she can never come back to him.

If you can make it incontrovertibly clear that when your daughter leaves you will back her without equivocation, it will help. Especially if you have demonstrated your loyalty consistently through the years, you have a fighting chance. As part of your bargain, insist that she not go back until her abusive mate gets professional help and demonstrates that he really has changed.

When Your Child Has Psychological Problems

Wendy left home when she was sixteen, couldn't get along with her mother. Cheyenne, Wyoming, was too small for her and we just thought she had an unbridled urge to see the world. Now I don't know.

Sometimes we'd get a card from San Francisco or a collect call from San Diego and she sounded fine. We could never reach her except sometimes when she'd give us the address of a hotel she was working in, something like that. She never did bother us for money, though.

Then about two years ago she called us up from New York and said she and this young man, Earl, were married. Mother cried a lot that night, she kind of had in mind a traditional wedding. Earl sounded sort of nice on the phone. As soon as Wendy started fussing with Mother here, he got on and said, "Is that my new mother-in-law? Hi there, Mom." And he saw to it we got lots of pictures of the wedding. It was outdoors, in somebody's garden, and his father, a baker, had made them the wedding cake.

That first Thanksgiving we sent them tickets to come and visit. It was the first time in five years we'd seen Wendy and we thought she looked mighty fine. Different in her ways from her mother and me, but like I told my wife, what did you expect? Her husband seemed to care for her, had his arm around her a lot, and that made us feel kind of good, like maybe she was finally settling down. He's a gym teacher in a high school out there, and, frankly speaking, I was surprised she married such a steady and educated person.

Now I don't know what to think. Yesterday we got a call from a hospital and you could've knocked me over. This doctor said he was a psychiatrist and Wendy was there and he wanted us to come to New York. When we asked about Earl, the doctor said he had left her.

He said, "Mr. Smith, your daughter says she heard voices telling her to kill her husband, and that's what she tried to do."

I said, "Is it serious?"

The doctor said, "It's serious. You better come."

Psychological problems often show up during childhood or adolescence but sometimes they don't surface until marriage or childbirth. It can truly come as a shock to you that your child's divorce is connected with bizarre behavior. If, like Wendy, your child threatens murder or suicide, or displays any other dangerous symptoms, you must give and get help immediately. Most important is competent medical care. If he or she is in treatment, make certain that the therapy and medication are continued even if you have to foot some of the cost. If there is no treating therapist, find the best available professional for the particular illness. You may opt to get therapy for yourself and other family members, not to play up your guilt and self-blame, but to find out as much as you can about how to interact positively.

Some parents we interviewed had children who had been hospitalized prior to divorce. Interestingly, it was usually the hospitalized child rather than his or her mate who initiated the divorce. Other parents we interviewed felt that their divorcer needed psychiatric help and refused to get it. Only when there is clear indication of potential harm to self or others can psychiatric care or hospitalization be legally ordered.

One parent, Mrs. Williams, described how upsetting it was to get unexpected long distance phone calls at 2:00 or 3:00 A.M. from her divorced daughter, Madge, who either cried or called her names. She begged her daughter to get help, and when the calls got worse she enlisted the assistance of the police and went for her. Shortly afterward, that mother and daughter started therapy together. It wasn't an easy road for either of them. Sometimes Madge threatened her mother's life and sometimes she threatened to take her own, but the therapy paid off. Mrs. Williams broke down and confessed that Madge's father, whom Madge had never seen, lived in the psychiatric ward of a veterans' hospital. Madge went to California to meet him and now she is working out her angers and finding new ways of dealing with them. Her mother is relieved that she is doing better, has a part-time job, and is going out with friends. Mrs. Williams is sleeping through the nights. No more 2:00 A.M. phone calls.

Yes, Even Criminality

Sometimes I am bitter and I ask God, "Why did you send my son to prison?" What did he do? Income tax evasion? Everybody cheats on income taxes, but my son got caught. Sometimes I blame my son. I am mad at him for being stupid enough to get caught; other times I just feel sorry. He's my baby and I imagine what he's suffering up there with all those Big Timers. I try to visit him, and send him packages and letters, because one thing I know I won't write him off the way that bitch did. She [his wife] stuck around and enjoyed all the fun with that tax money, but where is she now? The last he heard from her was through her lawyer.

Chances are this is not the first bad news that distraught mother had about her child. It is likely that you too had already lived through some nightmares with your son or daughter. You hoped his arrests for stealing and using someone else's credit card, or her probation for shoplifting, were history and that marriage was a chance for a fresh start. Maybe your in-law knew about the past; maybe not. You felt relieved that your child was out there on his own, that he or she was now someone else's responsibility. But you can't always get off the hook that easily.

You were hoping that all the dread and heartache were past, and then, one Monday night, it's, "Hi, Mom and Dad. What's for supper?" and your heart knows that something is rotten in the marriage. When you hear the word *divorce* your grief is probably especially intense. You are angrier, guiltier, more ashamed than the average parent.

One response, of course, is total despair, but don't give in to it. Before you give up, get the facts if you can. Criminal indictment merits a day in court according to our system of law, so give your child his day to be heard. The first distressing reports will probably come not from your child but from the victims. No matter what the offense, you cannot wipe your child out of your life. You must find ways to understand, plan, and act. As difficult as it is, you must hear the whole story.

We don't recommend a too-quick invitation to move back home while his case is being resolved. He needs to face up to the consequences of his behavior. Offering a safe harbor with no strings attached—no questions asked, no demands made—is carrying loyalty too far. Being there for your child by no means calls for condoning his or her behavior, but it may mean supplying bail, sitting through deeply painful court sessions, and ultimately facing his or her imprisonment. Once more, we recommend therapy. If the lawyer can persuade the judge to make psychiatric help a condition of your child's sentence, that would be optimum. Whether it is your son or daughter wh is in prison, visit him or her as often as possible, write, and send packages. Keep in close touch.

If there are grandchildren, you must help them accept the way things are. Take them with you when you go to see your child. That is more desirable than pretending that mom or dad is just away for a while. It is almost always a good idea to be open, truthful, and supportive with your grandchildren, rather than secretive. A direct approach is easier for them to deal with. They have to know they can trust what you are telling them, and they will respect you for it. This doesn't mean that you discuss everything in front of your grandchildren. How you answer their questions depends on their age, personality, and what they can handle.

Bad Seed, Bad Idea

Divorce is rarely easy, but divorce with dark undertones challenges even the strongest parent. If your ex-law is an addict (alcohol or drug), mentally ill, abusive, or in prison, your child may feel that you don't want your grandchildren exposed to the ex-law's family.

Many of the people we interviewed had this specific recommendation for parents who give shelter to their desperate child and frightened grandchildren. Now that you know what they have lived through for many years, you are probably determined to protect them. In fact, we hope you do (unfortunately, many parents still believe in the till-death-do-you-part axiom and turn their child away). Protection is paramount, but don't cut off contact with your ex-law's entire family—the other set of grandparents, the other aunts and uncles, and even cousins. Don't adopt a Bad Seed attitude—that the family is tainted. We do not question the need for extreme measures to protect your grandchildren from further harm. However, these do not necessarily involve shunning the entire other side of the family.

Ultimately, it is your child's decision, not yours, whom the grandchildren relate to, but if you are living in a three-generation household for the present, your point of view matters. Keep in mind that your grandchildren will benefit from a variety of love relationships (don't we all?). They need to know their roots, the more so when they reach adolescence and struggle with issues of identity. If your child cuts off a whole arm of his children's family, the youngsters are mystified, curious, and worried that there's a bad part of themselves they're forbidden to acknowledge. To permit them to know and ask questions about the "other side" is to give them a chance to learn to deal with it. It is more than a question of identity, it is the foundation of mental health.

A grandparent from Ohio argues: "But you don't know what it's like with my grandchildren after a visit with their other kin. It stirs them up. They misbehave and it takes days to calm them down, especially the older one." Children can't put all the turmoil aside and forget it. They must be permitted to talk about it, unpleasant as it might be. You can help your grandchildren sort out their experiences; if they are too sordid and unpleasant, they will reject them themselves. It is not uncommon for children who are forbidden contact with their other parent's family to grow to be like that other parent. Perhaps it is the only way these children can find to achieve the closeness they yearn for.

General Guidelines for Coping

1. Confront the situation and refrain from words of condemnation until you have heard the whole story.
2. Take a stand that will require you and your child to face the problem.
3. Hammer out with your husband or wife what stand you

will take in concert. Discuss it again and again. If you can't agree, abide by one decision, together.

4. Keep a balance between being supportive and tough love.

5. Seek counsel for yourselves from an attorney, a physician, a religious leader, or a therapist. In some instances you will need them all.

6. Seek a support group that handles the specific anxieties confronting you.

7. Strongly encourage your child to find a professional who specializes in whatever difficulty he or she is experiencing.

8. Don't consider it a sign of weakness if your child seeks his own counselors without consulting you. Above all else, this is evidence that he or she wants to change.

9. Step into the situation only when your child or ex-law cannot handle the care of your grandchildren.

10. Finally, recognize that the terrible eruption might save and/or change your child's life, move him or her into understanding himself or herself, and give you new perception and insight.

10

"Mom, Dad, I'd Like You to Meet . . ."

Here We Come, Ready or Not

Can I really find room in my heart for my son's second wife or my daughter's third husband?

You might as well get used to the idea of serial marriages, they are here to stay. It might be that you have already met your son's next wife or your daughter's future husband. This prospective spouse could have been in the picture even before the red divorce flag went up and your family went on alert. However, you can't assume that the divorce is the result of the interference of a homebreaker, "the other man/woman." The affair your son or daughter had during marriage might have only been transitional, a symptom of malaise in the marriage and a symbol of his or her struggle to get out of it. After a while you will meet the new flame and wonder if this man or woman will one day call you "Mom 'n' Dad."

Perhaps after the separation your son met someone attractive at a business conference, or your daughter gave her phone number to the man she sat next to on the plane as she was flying home to tell you her marriage was over. Whatever the romantic circumstance, you have to face the fact that your child is in a more resilient moment of his life than you are. He may be grief-stricken, but he can go on to the next step while you may still be mourning his last misadventure or fearful of the next one. No matter what the situation, it is more than likely that your divorcer will start dating again before there is a legal stamp on the separation.

A mother cries, "How many times can I go through this? After Ralph's marriage to Betty—the first time for them both—it took me quite a while before I could settle her into my heart as one of the family. Yesterday he brought this new woman to us, and I think he is serious about her. I just hope he doesn't rush into anything. It's too soon for him, I think, and I know it's too soon for us!"

You may feel like that. Making room for a new family member takes work: talking, measuring, looking, overlooking. It is different from the first time your child married. You may have lost confidence that she can tell what is right for her. After all, you have seen that she hasn't exercised the most astute judgment in choosing a mate or working through the travails of marriage before. You may feel that you are not ready to accept a new child, but nobody is asking you if this is the right moment for your family to expand.

A thirty-year-old lawyer, thinking about the possibility of a second marriage, reflected on her parents' acceptance:

> I suppose I hope they will like whomever I marry next. It is impossible for them not to be pleased. They hated the same things in Ed that I didn't like, and I won't marry that kind of man again. In that sense, their approval means a lot to me. I have decided that some things are more important to me than I had thought they were before, and that, ultimately, has much to do with what is important to them.

That declaration makes clearer than a thousand pictures how strongly young adults feel about parental approval. The following statement shows a mother's not uncommon ambivalence, uncertainty, and anxiety:

> Now I am angry with my son. He's living with a girlfriend. She's a nice girl and I like her because she is nice to my granddaughter. Actually, I don't have any feelings for her. In the beginning I was happy for him. I said, "I don't want you to be alone, but I don't want to see your girlfriend." I am still not ready to socialize. I was rude and cold to them when he brought her over. She was offended and left. So did he. I can't help it.

Like that mother, you are confused about meeting a possible new in-law. Your child has memories of how easily and fully you accepted her first husband, or how much you disapproved of him. The recollection makes her nervous either way. She still wants your approval, wants you to love yet another child. But you are still hurting from the sense of loss and grief over the divorce.

> Before my daughter finally remarried she brought many boyfriends home for dinner, and after a while I just accepted them as friends. When she remarried three years later I had no trouble with her new husband, but I know now he'll always be a son-in-law, never a son.

Fathers, as well as mothers, are filled with doubt, caught up in memories of a loving relationship now gone. "I'm afraid to love Cyndy, the new one. I gave my daughter-in-law a lot of love and respect. She was a fine woman and belonged in our family. I don't know how I'd take it if I let myself feel that way about this one and then lost her too."

Your child's venture into the singles' world sends you into a watchful, wondering frame of mind. A mother of a separated son said to her husband, "He's an attractive man. I notice there are single women happy to invite him to dinner, act as his hostess at parties, help decorate his apartment. I hope he is wary." *Wary*—that's what you are, about the whole business of a possible new mate for your child.

If your divorcer is a woman, your concerns are much the

same as when she was younger, about the traps ahead for her, about the dangers of promiscuity. You can't stomach the idea of her going from bed to bed, women's liberation notwithstanding. One mother had happily watched her daughter put her life back together after divorce, get a good job, go to singles' parties, and seek a support group. When a man moved in with her, Mom began to balk. That seemed going too far. But when Mom's friends accepted him as her child's partner, she found the situation easier to live with. She even conceded that a trial period of living together might be a good idea rather than a hasty marriage. Give yourself license to feel comfortable with your child's live-in mate.

One father, ashamed that his son had left his wife and four children for a co-worker almost twenty years his junior, said, "I hope he has his fling and then goes home to his family. What does a young girl want with a married man so much older? As for him, I guess he is in his mid-life something or other." That father never got the answer he wanted. His son went on to get a divorce and married "the young girl."

Part of the reason for the uneasiness of these parents is the fear that if their child rushes into a commitment too fast, it seems to imply that their divorcer was the one eager to be rid of the marriage, not willing to work at it. They blame their son or daughter for the breakup and have those old uneasy feelings that they, as parents, are guilty too. Don't put yourself through that.

Sex and Singlehood

It is likely that your children are as uneasy about dating, new mates, and AIDS as you are. Your daughter speculates about when and if she should have sex with the men she sees. If she has children, she may hesitate to invite her dates into the house after a night out. Your son, grown and once married, thinks about the same old things he did when he went out with girls in earlier days: whether she will like him, and whether it's a good idea to go to bed on the first date. At this point, the need of divorcers to go to bed is more a search for affirmation of their desirability and proof of their sexuality than an expression of love or a fulfillment of sexual desire. Divorce is often all rejection; affirmation that what your child often suspected during an uneasy marriage was true—that he or she was unloved, not lovable. What a tempting way to prove oneself worthy of love by jumping into a seductive scene. "Somebody wants me!" There is evidence of less promiscuity since the fear of AIDS has pervaded the whole country.

You are certainly interested and curious about this in-between period that could lead to remarriage. Many of you are still skeptical that divorce and mate-changing are better than life-time commitment, that your child will really be happier than before. Sure, you are concerned, but affecting your child's choice is another matter. You probably cannot.

While your child is single again you are of two minds. You don't want him to be lonely, but you don't want him to rush into a new marriage on the rebound. If you call and find him home, you start seeking out friends with eligible daughters. If you call him and don't get an answer, you worry that he is being promiscuous. The same doubts and wishes apply to you whose daughters are between marriages. You mail clippings of singles' events to her, and yet you hope she won't remarry in haste out of loneliness. Experience and research tell you that is a dangerous route to take. If your daughter remarries to make up for her hatred of her former spouse or because she was hurt by him, she is taking a risk. If your son is basing his decision on negatives (going from), rather than positives (going toward), that may augur trouble.

You are uncertain about your own emotions, too. How many times can you go through the process of accepting the women he is "serious" about? How many times can you look at the latest "candidate" and try to prejudge how she will fit into your family mobile, only to find she is no longer your son's one and only? You do get cynical after a while. The alternative is to ask him not to bring them home to you until he is thinking of settling in with one, but that may keep him away from some family events you wish him to attend.

Acceptance of your son's new woman, even if she doesn't become his wife, or of your daughter's new man, even if she never marries him, gives your child a much-needed sense that he or she can choose well, that you do have confidence in his or her judgment. Telling your child not to bring any friends home cuts you off from him. Better to think each new date is just that and enjoy her.

This suddenly single child of yours feels empty, like half a person. Separation leaves a void, and many divorcers need to fill it quickly. Your child, consciously or not, wants to prove that someone else loves him in spite of whatever rejection he has just suffered.

Should you welcome your son's new friend into your home during the separation period? Aside from your own feelings, consider those of your ex-law. One divorcee, in the throes of postseparation isolation, screamed, "My husband has a new girlfriend, and my in-laws' acceptance is so quick and open I'm furious about it." Of course, you don't want to disappoint your son or arouse his resentment by refusing to meet his "latest," but if you suspect your early approval of her will escalate the anger between him and his wife, you should discuss it with him. It could make the divorce settlement more difficult between them, and it could make your ex- (his ex-) vengeful about you.

Most parents we interviewed were more curious than cautious about meeting their divorcer's newest potential partner. You, too, will probably prefer to have a chance to get to know this new person before any wedding plans are set. This may or may not happen. According to statistics, chances are your child will pick a fellow divorcer. He won't like to think he needs your approval, but underneath all that bravado, your okay will matter.

Do You Like Him? Does He Like You?

All parties are nervous at the meeting between a likely spouse and possible in-laws. You and he are cautious, your daughter is tense. She does want you to like him. You may feel he is just the same as the last one, or just the opposite. She hopes you will accept him and that he will like you. You may feel that you are betraying your ex-law by being cordial to the new one, and you may be dubious about how long this relationship will last. You have been burned once and are going to be pretty careful about extending your love to this suitor. One mother said, "Truthfully, this boyfriend doesn't mean a thing to me. I don't care if I never see him again in my whole life. But I realize that she is going to make her life with him, and if I want any relationship with her, I have to. Otherwise, I could lose her completely, which I don't want to happen. It's enough I've lost Alan, my son-in-law."

Before they had gotten over the shock of separation and divorce, the Fiore's son brought a woman, much younger than his ex-, to meet Mom and Dad. Mrs. Fiore remembers that Rosa, the newcomer, asked, almost before the amenities were over and the quick appraisal had begun, "What work do you do?" "I work for the city," said Mom. "I'm a paralegal," countered Rosa. Mrs. Fiore commented to us, "How different from my meeting with my mother-in-law-to-be, twenty-eight years ago. I was quite respectful and careful, asked no questions, only answered them—all four hundred. It felt like the third degree! Of course, there were lots of queries about my family and my homemaking abilities. It was a different time. Yet, I liked Rosa for her directness and was pleased that she assumed I had a job. That seemed important to her. We were testing each other."

You are wary over many aspects of this next marriage. You know your child's performance as a mate. You are afraid she will fail again. You wonder, will you ever be able to accept this man, love him? (There's a good chance you will.) Will he find you wanting? (In some ways, yes, in others, no.) Do you like him as much as the last one? (Give him time.) What kind of family does he come from? (You don't have to love them.) Will he want children? (Will she?)

You are not sure what your feelings are. You certainly come to it with emotions different from your response to the first wedding. Then, the bride and groom were younger, untried, embarking on what you saw as a lifelong adventure. This couple will be following many familiar routes and charting new ones. You may have trouble getting quite as enthusiastic or excited as you did before. You don't think you will invite so many friends and relatives to the wedding this time around. You may even feel embarrassed over the thought that there is an implied pressure on your friends to send yet another gift to your child. Don't be concerned about that. They could be hurt if you don't invite them. What they do about a gift is up to them.

If your child senses that you are unhappy with her choice and asks you for reasons, that may mean she has some reservations too. They may be the same as yours or different. You can ask what she thinks, and after she has said her piece, and she wants to hear your thoughts, tell her without being harsh. This can make for an open discussion. You could ask, "Does he hope to change you?" (Look out.) "Do you want him to change?" (Ditto above.) "Is he controlling, flexible, rigid?" (Flexible is good.) Of course, you both are wondering how it will work out, and neither can give any answers with surety. In spite of such open discussions and love, one divorcee expressed it well when she spoke of her gratitude to her parents: "They are there to talk to and give me emotional support and they always will be. I know I can count on them. I need that. But the emotional support is quite different from approval of decisions I make." (Hear, hear!)

Grandchildren

You wonder what kind of stepparent the newcomer will be and how the children will feel about her. If the new mate has children, can you accept them? Take heart, most grandparents have few problems with stepgrandchildren, and the young ones may be counting on their fingers how many more holiday and birthday gifts they can expect under the new arrangement.

Acceptance, Try It

More than ten years ago, Dr. William Kephart reported, "In less than three years following an unhappy marriage and the divorce, two-thirds of all women and three-fourths of all men remarry. Those who remarry show a marked tendency to marry someone in a similar marital status . . . a divorced man will marry a divorced woman. Furthermore, those who divorce in the United States show a tendency to marry someone from a different religion."*

It may throw you that your in-law has a different set of holidays from those you have always celebrated. Usually, parents prefer that their child marry someone of similar background. This does make some things easier; values, holidays, etc., but differences are stimulating if you don't resist them. It could be fun to participate in new rituals and prepare untried, exotic dishes for family feasts. This mother describes some of her feelings in the matter:

My daughter married this really nice Jewish boy. They had both been married before. Sally has two children already, my grandchildren. Dave has a son. The kids seem to get along fine as far as I can see. Sally's two daughters are six and eight. Dave's son is only four. The girls take care of him like little mothers. It's cute to see. Sally is going for an M.B.A. and Dave is proud of her. The girls are in school all day and Dave's son, Billy, goes to preschool. It is a good, if mixed, family. Dave is a good father.

I had trouble at first on holidays. I wasn't sure Dave and Billy

*The *Family, Society and the Individual,* (Houghton Mifflin, 1977.)

would eat my Christmas ham. I was a little cautious about eating the noodle pudding Dave's mother sent me. (It was delicious.) The kids celebrate all the holidays, Dave's and ours. I haven't been to Passover at their house yet. I hope I'll know what to do.

I am learning to eat lox and bagels. But there are more differences between families than food.

How you receive this new member into your family is up to you. Nowadays life is change all the way. Unless you choose to stay frozen in the past, you must move and grow. This new marriage will bring new relatives and friends. It could mean vegetarian meals at times (and in-laws of a different color and/or culture), certainly new faces at your table. Whatever your thoughts, it is the decision of your child. He sees it as positive. You don't have to agree with all of it, but you do have to accept the fact of the marriage, since almost all divorced men and women remarry in these times.

Sons, Daughters, and Remarriage

Parents seem to wish for a daughter's remarriage more than for a son's. You would like someone to take care of her, to wipe the lost, searching look from her eyes, to help by being a father to her children, if there are any. Your hopes for remarriage may extend to your daughter-in-law. This could be sympathy, guilt, shame, or relief that someone other than your son will be responsible for her. If she has custody of your grandchildren, you might feel it would be healthier for them to have a live-in father in addition to one who merely visits. Her life might be easier and therefore life for your grandchildren would be better.

You may also feel good when your ex-son-in-law remarries. Perhaps you thought your friends were labeling your family "troubled." Our friends' responses to our lives are important to most of us. We all like to be thought of as successful; as people, parents, and as a family. When each member of the ex-couple becomes part of the "marrieds" again—still an ideal in our world—as opposed to "divorced," which is a stigma among many groups, you will feel that your friends will see your family as "normal" once more. You will like saying to them, "They are all very happy."

It seems that more men remarry than women. They have a wider field to choose from. They marry younger women more often than women marry younger men. The tradition still lingers that men can easily go out and aggressively seek a mate. Many women are still reluctant to appear to be looking for men. They go to the theater, to restaurants, and on vacations alone or with other women. Often they would like to ask a man out, but it is not yet comfortable for them to do so.

There is also a growing number of women who don't want to remarry. Some women seem not to need the benefits of remarriage as much as men do. Yet, being self-sufficient is a lonely road. They miss the intimacy of marriage. They long for warmth and closeness. They liked not having to think about whom to do things with, from seeing a movie to going to bed. Some women, like this one, opt for living with a man rather than marriage:

> I don't want to get married again, at least not right now. I need time to get my head on straight. I haven't really gotten over the last one yet. I'm not sure what went wrong with our marriage. It seemed so good for a while. Well, it's over. I've been dating again, but that is just a game, figuring out how quickly you'll hop into bed and out again.
>
> I can't imagine making a commitment to any of the men I know now. Two of them I like, but then I like my freedom, too. Sometimes I think maybe I'd like to live by myself during the week and just have a weekend relationship; someone romantic but without too many strings attached. Other times I am lonely. I get tired of having to plan every evening. Maybe if I wanted a baby, I'd get married again, but right now I'm just looking for someone to live with without the "I do's."

Like this woman, many couples formed of previous divorcers need a part-time relationship. Usually this is a temporary need, born of burnt-out emotions, distrust, and caution, and in time both parties want more of each other. Occasionally, a part-time relationship suits the temperamental—rather than temporary— need for distance of both partners. Some people definitely prefer distance in their relationships. Your child may go through many variations of testing the degrees of commitment during the transitional time after divorce.

Part-time or live-in relationships may be confusing for you to handle. Fathers may find it hard to sit in the same room with their daughter's "lover." Mothers may laugh nervously when they refer to their son's live-in relationship. Introducing her to friends can be awkward. One mother blurted out, "You know Vanessa, Herb's whatchamacallit." Usually parents take their cue from their child as to how much they invite this undefined partner to their home to family celebrations. Likewise, they adopt a wait-and-see attitude about inviting him into their heart.

Down the Aisle Again

Sooner or later most of you will have to be part of another wedding. This one may be less grand than the first, or more lavish, depending on who is in charge. You may ponder the wording of the invitations or just plain call a few relatives and friends to join you. Clergy from two different religions might officiate, or perhaps a judge. The second time around, you are likely to have less of a hand in the arrangements. Your daughter and her groom are more mature, more experienced, than they were at their respective first weddings, so they will probably cue you in on the invitations and attire.

The wedding invitations, if you have them, can read:

Mr. and Mrs. John Doe
Request the pleasure of your company
at the marriage of their daughter
Mrs. Anne Doe (maiden name) Smith (divorced name)

If the bride wants to wear white, it's her wedding. You can wear long, short, tux/tails, or a business suit, whatever seems appropriate. Weddings are shared proof of intent and celebrations of commitment. The key words for you are *share* and *celebrate*.

As to the question of wedding pictures, it is time to put away (not throw away) the old ones, and get the frames ready for new ones. Don't put the old ones too far away. Your grandchildren may want to look at them from time to time. For you they are part of the family history that shaped your ever-changing mobile. Your wedding gift to the new couple can be luxurious or practical or both. It depends on how much you can afford and how much you feel like giving, whether the gift is stocks, bonds, a check, or a set of dishes. Your son or daughter may make a comparison with the gift you gave the last time around the marriage-go-round, but that is his or her problem. Gifts express the giver.

Children of the bride or groom or both will be at the ceremony. These young ones may need special ministrations during the festivities. They desperately want to feel part of it all, but could act up out of uncertainty as to where they belong and what all the excitement has to do with them. For their sake, and of course for your child's, enter into the spirit of the occasion wholeheartedly. You may wonder if your tears this time are signs of mourning for the marriage that is over or for your fear that this one may dead-end, too. You may not take a second or third marriage with as much hope as you did the first, but it marks a significant step for the couple, more momentous, perhaps, than the first wedding.

Sisters, Cousins, Aunts

Your parents and relatives will, of course, want to meet the new bride or groom. They feel the imbalance of the family mobile. How you present your new in-law to them will help their initial reaction. "Our new son/daughter" makes matters clear as to your expectation for the union. The relatives, like you, will be curious, wary, but they will take their cue from you. Chances are they will be happy that your child is married again.

Settling In

Adopting a new in-law may not seem easy in prospect, but after some family meals, outings shared, and matters discussed, there will emerge a sense of intimacy that will dispel the strangeness. The new figure on the mobile may not seem to hang as firmly yet as the one it replaces, but he or she is there, and some family balance is restored. Your family is expanding. The empty seat at the table is filled again.

You may be thinking about your grandchildren and how they feel after the gala wedding settles into a live-together marriage. A grandmother was visiting when her eight-year-old grandson had invited a friend home from school. "How many dads do you have?" Sam asked. "One, of course." The grandson boasted, "I'm lucky. I have two."

Those "Other Parents" Again

On the way to the remarriage you may have felt anxious about yet another set of in-law parents. You may have thought they did not approve of their son or daughter marrying a divorced person. Some parents are upset by that, but, as we said earlier, there is a good chance that their child is also divorced.

You could find in them a sympathetic mirror-response to your anxieties about the new family. In any case, the likelihood is that you will see less of them than you did of the first set, but that does not rule out cordiality. You may even like them. You will probably share grandchildren. Both sets of parents are more than likely guarded in their response to the new in-law child and to his or her parents. After all, there is a kind of déjà vu in these ritualistic encounters.

Steps . . . Mother, Father, Family

In the divorce process, a family is said to collapse, when in reality it often expands. There are all those "steps"—stepparents, stepchildren, stepgrandparents. Elizabeth Einstein (*The Stepfamily, Living, Loving, Learning*) says that half the children born in the 1970s will live in broken families and most will become stepchildren; that there are more than 25 million stepfamilies and 1,300 new ones forming every day. In a classroom we visited in suburban Philadelphia, not one child comes from an intact family. The child of divorce is no longer an exception at home or in school, but many youngsters are nonetheless self-conscious about not having both "real parents."

When your son remarries he is beset with new kinds of family challenges, different from those he had in his first marriage. If his new wife has children, he feels that they are constantly measuring him against their "real dad." He and his new wife have to decide whether he should be "the heavy" when it comes to disciplining the children (it usually takes the children two years to accept his authority) or just leave that to their mother. If his former wife has custody of his children, he will tend to make the hours he is with them a celebration, special-treat time, to compensate for the time he is away. If your daughter gets stepchildren as part of her new marriage package, she has to combat the Cinderella story image of the wicked stepmother. She has to prove that she in no way resembles that evil witch. We may need a new name for stepmother. The French call a stepmother *belle mere*. In addition to having to refute a fairy tale image, your daughter is facing the challenge of living in a house with partially grown children to whom she is expected to be the nurturer. She probably had a good bit of exposure to them during the courtship period and has experienced some of the rearing problems and decisions, but it is different now. She is a full-time mother for children who may resent her and are surely making comparisons with the "real mom."

We spoke to Sandy, a newly married divorcee. She had great confidence in the bachelor who got a "package deal" of wife, children, home, and Little League just by saying, "Marry me."

At age thirty-eight, Alvin believed it was too late to start the family he'd always wanted, and this ready-made trio suited him completely. He was tender and loving to the children, and when they needed discipline Sandy felt that since he was given the privilege of loving them he had to set limits for them, too.

When your grandchildren become part of a new family combination, they will be charting its successes and failures daily. If they are under age ten, their adjustment will be easier than if they are on the edge of adolescence or already in their teens. If your older grandchildren have to move from their accustomed neighborhood and enter a new school, such changes and the business of finding new friends are often disturbing. Certainly, taking on a new parent is hard for them to handle. It is especially unnerving at a time when their incipient adulthood pushes them to emotionally move away from their family, old or new, to be more on their own, and then to come back to be nurtured. They want both in and out of parental protection at this stage. To have also to measure the acceptability of a new parent at this ambivalent time of their lives is rough on them.

They will be jealous of the attention paid the new parent by the old. If theirs is a blended family, with two sets of children, rivalries will be simmering beneath the surface and out on the domestic battlefield. "We never used to have to eat everything on our plates." "What did you get? I didn't get the bike I wanted." "Your name is different from ours." However, sibling rivalry is not new to your grandchildren unless they were "onlies."

If your grandchildren don't get to see you as often as they once did, don't be surprised. For one thing, they now have more grandparents to visit. You must also face the fact that the new stepmother or stepfather is not sure how much of a meddler you are. You may be kept at arm's length for a while. Move slowly. The press of everyone's getting used to the new living arrangements takes time. Keep the connections open. You are a very important link to the past for these children. Don't be critical, even if the rules are changed for them and for you. Stand nearby. Your grandchildren may want your lap and your ear for pouring out their complaints. "She doesn't let me . . . He makes us . . ." Listen, but don't comment. Learn what changes and new rules operate in this new family. The extended family—your relatives—can help too. Everyone has to give this new blend time to figure out how and with whom to celebrate holidays, and whom they choose as special out of the increased numbers of kinfolk.

If you get stepgrandchildren in the change, make room for them in your lap, too. This woman does: "My ex-daughter-in-law has two children with her new husband. When I go to Ohio to visit my granddaughter I am 'Gramma' to all the children in the household. Once the older boy said, in anger, to his brother, 'She's not your real grandma, don't call her that.' The reply was, 'But she looks like one. She's Annie's real one, and besides, she sends us Christmas presents.' " When you are with these "adopted grandchildren" and meet a friend, it is good to introduce them as your grandchildren, unless they object or you are uncomfortable. Then introduce them simply by their names.

Family Is Still a Good Word

With all the tolerance and forbearance you are being asked to muster, you must know, too, that you are entitled to your pain and grief responses. There comes a time when you have to put them away. There are few occasions more satisfying than gathering your grown children and their families to your table and enjoying the fruits of a job well done. We do like to feel successful as parents, to see our family expand. There is a glow that warms us when our child is happily paired and settled in a good relationship. Whether or not you weep over the broken marriage, keep in mind that your child will likely try again. This one could be forever.

ABOUT THE AUTHORS

Dorothy Weiss Gottlieb majored in journalism at Temple University. After a career with a management consulting firm, she joined forces with a forensic psychiatrist at the University of Pennsylvania to develop multi-disciplinary programs on law and psychiatry. She has published a number of papers in professional journals and has established nationwide contacts with psychiatrists, psychologists, lawyers and judges, sociologists, and social workers. She has two sons and two granddaughters.

Inez Bellow Gottlieb holds a B.A. in Sociology and an M.A. in Communications from the University of Pennsylvania. She has recently retired from her twenty-year career as a network programming executive. Her work as an executive producer has won her many honors and awards, including an Emmy, The Cine Golden Eagle, and The Eudora Welty Award. She has three children and five grandchildren.

Marjorie Slavin, M.S.W., majored in social science at Sarah Lawrence College, holds a Masters degree in Social Work from New York University, and received her Certificate in Family Therapy from the Hunter College Postgraduate Clinical Program. She currently has a private practice in Riverdale, NY, and also is affiliated with the Scarsdale Family Counseling Service. She has written numerous syndicated columns on relationships for newspapers and magazines. She has one son.